The Very Naughty
Joke Book

Father, I'm having wicked thoughts

The Very Naughty Joke Book

Tony Husband
and
Johnny Sharpe

ARCTURUS

ARCTURUS

This edition published in 2014 by Arcturus Publishing Limited
26/27 Bickels Yard, 151–153 Bermondsey Street,
London SE1 3HA

ISBN: 978-1-78212-469-6
AD003788UK

Printed in Malaysia

CONTENTS

RUGRATS

"Mummy, the milkman's here.
Are you going to pay him or shall
I go out to play?"

A woman was walking along the street with her little
daughter when they came upon two dogs humping.
When the daughter asked her mother what they were
doing, embarrassed Mum did some quick thinking
and replied, "The dog on top has hurt itself so the one
underneath is carrying it."
"Well, isn't that just typical?" said the little girl.
"You try to do someone a favour and all they do is turn
round and f*ck you."

A little girl in a convent school asks her
teacher, an old nun, who
came first, Adam or Eve.
"Adam," replied the nun. "Men always
come first."

Little Billy peeped into his big sister's bedroom one day to see her rubbing her hands between her legs, saying, "I need a man, God, I need a man."
The next night he peeped into her bedroom again and was amazed to find a man in bed with her. Later on that night if anyone had looked in Billy's room they would have seen him rubbing his hands between his legs, saying, "I need a PlayStation, God, please, I need a PlayStation."

'They seem a bit strict with their kids.'

A woman was breastfeeding her baby in the park when a young boy sat down next to her.
"What does the baby have to drink?" asked the boy.
"Just milk and orange juice," she replied.
After a few moments' thought, the little boy asked, "Which one is the orange juice?"

"Please Miss, I've hurt my finger," said little Rosie to her teacher.
"Have you got any cider?"
Puzzled, the teacher asked her why she wanted cider.
"Because I heard my sister telling her friend that when she gets a prick in her hand she always puts it in cider."

A little girl was found wandering down the crowded high street, crying her eyes out. When the policeman asked her what

was wrong, she told him she'd lost her father and was all on her own.
"What's your dad like?" he asked.
"Football, beer and fishing,"
she replied.

The parents were so proud when their son John went away to university, but all he did was constantly write home for money to spend on books, trips, membership fees and so on. Then halfway through the term he wrote to tell them he had a lead role in the university play but needed money for the costume.
All these demands for money were really beginning to annoy his parents, but they did as he asked. A month later he wrote to them again to say thanks.
"The party was fantastic," he wrote. "Everyone thought I looked a real count in the costume."
On seeing this, his father retorted, "Bloody hell, I give him all that money and he still can't spell!"

I always knew my parents really hated me.
My bath toys were a kettle and toaster.

At a family gathering, a young boy suddenly lets out a noisy fart.
"Bobby, manners please! You shouldn't do that in front of your grandma."
"Sorry, Dad, I didn't know it was her turn."

A concerned father knows that his son's pet hamster is dying and feels he ought to try to soften the blow.
"Son, I know your little Brownie is like one of the family, but eventually he will die and go up to heaven. We must try not to be too sad. He's had a good life with us, so we must celebrate the happy times and not get too upset when he goes."
The little boy takes all this in solemnly.
"Dad, can we have a party?"
"Yes, that's a good idea. You can invite some friends round."
"Dad?"
"Yes, son?"
"Can I kill him now?"

Two kids were arguing in the playground.
"My dad's a better darts player than yours," said the first boy.
"No, he ain't," said the second boy. "My dad got the highest score last week."
"OK, OK, but my mum's better than your mum."
"Yeah, alright, my dad says the same thing."

A very pompous self-made man decided to pay for his son to go to private school, and the whole family went up to visit the headmaster.
"I'm Sir Dunwell Bates, this is my wife Lady Bates, my daughter Miss Bates and my son Master Bates."
"Don't worry," replied the headmaster. "We'll soon put that right."

Neighbour to little girl: "What's the name of your new baby sister?"
Little girl: "I don't know. I can't understand a thing she says!"

Two women who had been at school together bump into each other ten years later. The first one is a bit of a show-off.

"Yes, I can't complain. I went for a job on an estate just outside Henley and ended up marrying the Lord of the Manor."

"Oh, how nice," says the second.

"And darling Jack encouraged me to start a stud farm and we've now got one of the best in southern England."

"Oh, how nice."

"We've got two lovely boys . . . at Eton, of course."

"Oh, how nice."

"Anyway, listen to me blathering on! What happened to you?"

"Me? Oh, I went to finishing school after we left, and learnt how to say, 'Oh, how nice' instead of 'F*ck you'."

"Cynthia," said the governess angrily, "it didn't look good when you let that strange man kiss you in front of the rest of the class."

"Well actually, Miss, it was better than it looked."

Two streetwise kids were walking to school when one said to the other, "Guess what? I found a condom on the patio."
The other replied, "What's a patio then?"

'OK, Tim, Mrs Booth is here for your piano lesson. Where have you hidden the piano?'

The local doctor was asked to give a talk on sex education to the girls at the local high school, but, knowing his wife was a bit of a prude, he told her he was speaking on hot-air ballooning. A few days afterwards the headmistress met the doctor's wife in the street. "Please tell the doctor again how much we enjoyed his talk. I think the girls learnt a lot from him."
"Well, I am surprised," exclaimed the wife. "He's only done it twice and the second time he couldn't get it up properly."

The student teacher was sitting in on a religious education lesson in Class 4B. Suddenly, the teacher turned to her and said, "Miss Lustleigh, will you tell the class the name of the first man."
"Well, I could," she replied coyly, "but I promised we'd keep it a secret."

A little boy was causing a great deal of trouble for the teachers. Each lunchtime, he would be taken to the dining room for dinner but, once there, he would refuse to sit down.
"Bollocks to you!" he would shout at the top of his voice, making all the other children behave badly as well. When he repeated this behaviour the following day, he was reprimanded but it didn't have much effect.
Again, he shouted, "Bollocks to you!" At the end of the week, his parents were contacted and told about his behaviour.
"Well, if that's how the little bugger acts, don't give him any dinner," replied Dad. "Bollocks to him!"

"Mummy, Mummy, the au pair is in bed with a strange man. Ha ha, got you! April Fool – it's only Daddy!"

QUIDS IN

The East End gang boss had always been very careful whom he employed, for fear of being grassed up. He thought he'd been really clever with his crooked accountant who was deaf and dumb. There wasn't much of a risk that he would overhear too much. However, it eventually dawned on the boss that someone was stealing money from him. A lot of money. And it didn't take long for him to discover that it was his crooked accountant.

"Benny," he ordered, "Get that b*stard down here pronto and get Marty to come with him. He understands sign language."

Later in his office, the boss started interrogating him.

"Marty, ask him what he's done with the money."

At first the terrified accountant signalled his ignorance of the theft but when a gun was put to his head, he spilled the beans. With rapid hand movements, he explained that he'd hidden all the money in a trunk in an old derelict factory, two miles from the office.

"So what did he say?" demanded the boss, impatiently.

"It's no good, boss," replied Marty. "He says you haven't got the bottle to shoot him, so you can go and get f*cked!"

A woman rings her husband up at work to tell him she's won the jackpot on the lottery and that he'd better start packing.
"Darling, that's wonderful!" he shouts with glee. "Where are we going?"
"I'm not bothered," she replied.
"Just make sure you're gone by the time I get home."

Bob suggested to his wife that a good way to save money would be to put £1 in the money box every time they made love.
A year went by and Bob decided to empty the box to see how much money had been saved. He couldn't believe his eyes when he found not only £1 coins but lots of £5, £10 and £20 notes as well.
"How come we've got all these notes?"
he asked, amazed.
"Well, not everyone's as stingy as you!"
his wife retorted.

A rich couple lost all their money, and were trying to think of ways to restore their fortunes. The husband said to his wife, "If you learnt to cook, we could get rid of the housekeeper."
And she retorted, "If you were better in bed, we could get rid of the gardener."

Flo's husband dies and because he was such a popular fella, she decides to put an announcement in the paper. But not having a lot of money, she tells the local newspaper she wants to keep it as short as possible.
"Just put 'Ben Potts dead'."
"Actually, Madam, you can have up to six words for the same price. Is there anything you would like to add?"
Flo thinks for a few moments, and then says, "Yes, OK, can you add, 'Ferret for sale'?"

Did you hear about the debutante who wrote home from the States to say she had a beautiful fur coat and it only cost her 200 bucks?
She never could spell!

The rich boyfriend presented his girlfriend with a beautiful fur coat made of skunk.
"I'm amazed," she said, "that such a gorgeous coat could come from such a stinking little beast."
"Well," said the boyfriend. "I didn't expect gratitude, but there's no need to get so personal!"

A woman has her portrait painted by a local artist and asks him if he would paint her dripping with fabulous jewels. She explains, "If I die before my husband and he gets married again, I want his second wife to go crazy looking for the stones."

The chairman turned to his secretary and said, "I'll never forget that weekend we spent together in the Cotswolds, will you?"
"I don't know," she replied, "it depends how much it's worth."

What's green and takes an hour to drink?
The family allowance cheque.

Was it love at first sight?
No, second.
The first time I didn't know he had so
much money.

'Money is short, okay?!!'

Three brothers are left their father's business in his will. The oldest son says, "Dad left me 48 per cent of the shares so I'm going to be chairman."

"OK," says the second son, "and I'll be in charge of the everyday running of the business because I've got 30 per cent of the shares."

"Now, wait a minute," says the third and youngest son. "What about me? Don't forget I've got 22 per cent of the shares."

The other two confer before turning back to their younger brother. "We've decided you can be in charge of sexual matters."

"What does that mean?"

"When we want your f*cking advice, we'll ask for it."

"It's no good, sir," said the DSS man to his interviewee. "You can't say you feel like 65 – you have to <u>be</u> 65."

A FAMILY AFFAIR

"Dad, Dad," said his son excitedly. "I've done it. I've got a part in the new play."
"Well done, lad, what is it?"
"I play an old man who's been married for 35 years."
"That's a promising start. Next time you might get a speaking part."

A man rushed into a newspaper office saying, "I hope I'm not too late to put an announcement in the paper – my wife has just given birth to a baby girl after ten years of trying."
"Of course, sir," replied the clerk. "How many insertions?"
"Oh, I can't remember – bloody thousands!"

"Mummy, Mummy, are little birds made of metal?"
"Of course not, darling, why do you think that?"
"I just heard Dad say he'd like to screw the a**e off the bird next door."

A simple-minded couple go to the doctor's because the wife is pregnant again with their fifth child in as many years.
"Why didn't you use the condoms that I instructed you to wear?" asked the doctor.
"I'm sorry, Doc," the man replied, "but we don't have an organ so I put it over the flute instead."

A very ugly couple were walking along the road with two beautiful children when they overheard a passer-by express amazement at the fact that two such ugly people could have such lovely children. They turned to the passer-by and said, "You imbecile, we didn't make them with our faces!"

A man is loading his kids into the car, five squeezed in the back and two in the front. As he gets in himself he's heard to mutter, "Wow, I almost screwed myself out of a seat!"

Two women were talking.
"My first pregnancy resulted in triplets and that only happens once every 250,000 times."
"Wow!" said her friend. "I'm surprised you ever had time to do any housework!"

It was decided to add sex education to the school curriculum and the parents were asked how they felt about this. The majority were in agreement with one proviso – no graphic demonstrations, just keep it oral.

"Look at this," said Flo's friend, holding up the newspaper.
"It says here that there are 19 women in the village all expecting a baby on the same day – June 23. Your baby's not due until July, is it?"
"No, it's not, but then I didn't go on the Mothers Union trip to Weymouth."

Just as the young girl is coming out of the school gates, a car draws up and a man leans over to ask if she'd like a lift home.
"No, thank you," she replies.
But he asks again.
"Come on, it's raining, you'll be soaked by the time you get home."
"No! Go away and leave me alone."
The man follows her up the road. "Look, get in please, I'll get you some sweeties."
"No!" she yells and starts to run.
"I'll get you some sweeties and your favourite comic."
"No, no, no!" shouts the girl. "Just because you bought the Skoda doesn't mean I have to ride in it, Dad."

A little girl went into her parent's bedroom to find her mum and dad in bed.
"Well!" she exclaimed. "And you tell me off just for sucking my thumb!"

Two husbands are in hospital anxiously waiting for their wives to give birth. One of them is so nervous that the other tries to comfort him, saying, "It'll be alright, mate, I've been through this before."
The nervous man asks a lot of questions, finally saying, "Can you tell me how long it will be before I can have sex with my wife again?"
"Are you private or NHS?"
"NHS."
"In that case, you'll have to wait until you get home."

'Erm... I think we've had enough sex for one marriage, don't you, Peter?'

"Hey, June, how about a bit of slap and tickle tonight?"
"Sshh, John, don't talk like that in front of the children.
Let's use code. Whenever you feel like it, just say, 'How
about turning the washing machine on.' "
A few evenings later, June turned to her husband and
said, "Shall I put the washing machine on tonight?"
"Don't bother, love, you looked a bit tired so I
did it by hand."

"Mummy, Mummy, what are you doing?"
exclaimed the little boy as he walked into
the bedroom to find her sitting on Daddy.
"Just flattening Daddy's tummy,"
Mum replied.
"I wouldn't bother, when you go out tonight
the au pair will only blow it up again."

My mother-in-law and I don't get along.
Take our anniversary for instance. She sent us some
monogrammed bath towels.
"Hers and Its."

The man at the bar looked sadly into his pint of beer and sighed heavily.
"What's up, Bob?" asked the landlord.
"It's my four-year-old son," the man said. "The little bugger's got our next-door neighbour pregnant."
"Get away!" exclaimed the landlord. "That's impossible."
"It's not. He punctured all my condoms with a needle."

"Now, son," said his father. "Let's see how much you've learnt in maths. What's two and two?"
After a moment the boy replied, "Four."
"Good," said his father, "but let's try to be a bit quicker. What's four and four?"
This time the boy counted on his fingers and replied, "Eight."
"OK," said Dad patiently, "but try not to use your fingers. Put your hands in your pockets. Now, what's five and five?"
After a few moments of fumbling the boy replied, "Eleven."

"Dad," said the young teenager, pointing to the condoms at the chemist's, "why do they come in different amounts?"
"Well, son," replied his dad, "the pack of three is for the lad who gets lucky at the weekends when he goes out clubbing. One for Friday and two for Saturday. Now the pack of six is for the experienced young bachelor who has a date nearly every day of the week. And finally, the pack of 12 is for the married man. One for January, one for February, one for March . . . "

"Geraldine, how could you?" exclaimed her mother, looking at paintings of her naked daughter hanging on the studio wall. "I can't believe you'd pose nude for your boyfriend."
"I didn't," she replied. "He must have painted them from memory."

The farmer and his wife are entertaining the local bigwigs when their son runs in and announces to his father in a loud voice, "Dad, Dad, the bull's f*cking the cow."

After a moment of shocked silence, the farmer turns to his son and calmly says, "Next time, son, be a little less explicit. You should have said, 'The bull is surprising the cow.' That sort of language comes from associating with riff raff."

Lo and behold, the following week the farmer and his wife are entertaining again when their son rushes in.

"Dad, Dad, the bull is surprising the cows."

"Well done, son, you've remembered what I told you, but you should have said the bull is surprising the cow . . . he can't surprise more than one cow at a time, you know."

"But he can, Dad!" insists the boy. "He's f*cking the horse."

Dad is mowing the lawn when his young son comes running out of the house calling to him.
"Daddy, Daddy, what's sex?"
For a moment Dad is dumbstruck, then he decides that if his son has asked the question, he must do his best to answer it.
For the next few minutes, Dad talks about the birds and the bees, human relationships, love, the sex act, having babies – in fact, he does a pretty good job of covering every aspect. Eventually he comes to a stop when he sees how oddly his son is looking at him.
"Why did you want to know?" he asks.
"Well, Mummy said to come out and tell you that dinner would be ready in two secs."

The little girl's mother was entertaining her next-door neighbour when her little daughter walked in.
"Hello, Mrs Crabbit, are you a gardening expert?" she asked.
"No, I'm not, why do you ask?" said the puzzled neighbour.
"Mum says if there's any dirt about you'll dig it up."

NEIGHBOURS

Two women talking over the garden wall. The first said,
"It's no good, Beryl, I'm at my wits' end. I can't stand the
sight of George any longer. He treats me like sh*t, he's
never at home, he just uses the place as a hotel and I
know he's sh*gging everyone in sight. It's had a terrible
effect upon me, I've already lost a stone in weight."
"Leave him, Sylvia, leave him and take him for everything
you can," replied her outraged friend.
"Oh, I will, I will. Just as soon as I lose another
half stone."

*A man looks over his garden wall to
see his neighbour digging a hole in the
back garden.*
"What are you up to?" he asks.
*"I'm digging a hole for my dead
hamster," he replies.*
*"Sorry to hear that, but it's a big hole
for a hamster, isn't it?"*
*"Of course it is, it's inside your f*cking
cat!" he yells.*

Two old men are chatting over the garden wall.
"I hear old Bates is living with a gorilla," says one.
"Well I never, is it male or female?"
"Female, of course. You know old Bates, there's nothing
unnatural about him."

*"Billy," said the blonde young neighbour.
"I forgot to get some milk at the
corner store, do you think you could go
for me?"
"No," said the boy, "but I overheard
Dad say he could."*

*'I told next door he would struggle
with his new hedge-cutter.'*

Two women are talking over the garden wall.
"You know, Doris, I've discovered a great way to get
more money out of my old man. Last week I wore a
low-necked jumper when we went shopping and as I
bent over the supermarket freezer one of my boobs
popped out. You should have seen Bill, he nearly
had a blue fit. I told him it was because I didn't have
enough money to buy a new bra, so he's increased my
housekeeping. You ought to try it for yourself."
The following week, the two women met up for another
chat and Doris was asked if she had taken her
friend's advice.
"Oh, it was a disaster!" exclaimed Doris. "We were just
about to go down the bingo when I lifted my skirt and
told my husband I had no knickers on because
I couldn't afford to buy any. The old skinflint, he
threw me a quid and told me to buy a comb.
'At least you can look tidy,' he said."

*"You're a fool to yourself, Ethel," said
her neighbour scornfully. "That husband
of yours has you running round in circles
after him."
"Oh don't say that," replied Ethel
with spirit.*

"He helps with the housework, you know. He sits in front of the television and gathers dust."

" . . . and another thing," continued the complaining woman, "I now know what eternity feels like. It's the time it takes between me coming and him leaving."

Three women were discussing safe sex. The first said she used the pill, the second said she always carried a packet of condoms and the third said she always used a tin with a few pebbles inside.
The other two looked at her in amazement.
"How does that work?" they asked.
"Oh, it's easy really. I get the man to stand on the tin and when I hear the pebbles start to rattle I kick it out from under him."

HER INDOORS

The woman went to the beauty parlour and after her treatment, said to the beautician, "Do you think my husband will think I'm beautiful?"
"I should think so. He still drinks a lot, doesn't he?"

The husband was standing on the crowded platform when he thought he saw his wife amongst the crowd. He pushed his way through the people, came up behind her and gave her a big hug and a lip-smacking kiss on the neck. To his horror, as the woman turned round, he realized it wasn't his wife. "Oh no, I'm so sorry," he said blushing profusely. "It's just that your head looks like my wife's behind."

Said the disillusioned woman, "The only time my husband wakes up stiff is when he's been jogging the night before."

"Colin," she whispered, nudging him
in the ribs to wake him up. "I can
hear noises downstairs, I think we've
got burglars. Go and see." But Colin
refused to move.
"What's happened to you?" she hissed.
"You were brave when you married me."
"I know," he replied, "that's what all my
friends said."

'Amazing, you've gone back into your family
400 years and they're all as boring as you.'

"Hello, Joan. You look happy today, what's going on?"
"Oh, Maisie, I am," she replied. "Last night my husband brought home a big tube of lubricant jelly. He said it would please me greatly.
And it did. When he went to the bathroom I smeared it all over the bedroom door and the silly sod couldn't get back in!"

The old woman turned sadly to her friend and said, "The spark's gone out of our marriage, Flo. These days, in bed, I bring out the animal in Alfred. He runs to the door, scratching and whining to get out."

After an hour of playing bridge and getting beaten every time, the husband excused himself to go to the bathroom. As he left the room, the wife turned to her hosts and remarked scornfully, "This'll be the first time I've known what's in his hand all night!"

Walter was hammering away in the garden when George popped his head up over the wall.
"Fancy a pint, Walt?" he asked.
"No, I can't," replied Walter sadly. "The wife's ill in bed, so I've got to look after her."
As if on cue, they heard terrible noises coming from the house.
"Is that her coughin'?" asked George.
"Don't be daft," replied Walter. "She couldn't get inside this. It's too small. It's going to be a new kennel for the dog."

'Darling, before you jump, can you find my collection of rare Beatles singles?'

A worried man went to the doctor's and asked him to come and visit his wife who was ill in bed with a bad chest infection.

"Just one thing in confidence, doctor," he said. "My wife never wears any knickers. I hate it. I beg her to change but she just won't listen to me. I wonder if you could somehow link her illness to her lack of underwear. Maybe it will convince her."

The doctor agreed and accompanied the man home. He examined the wife's throat and her chest very thoroughly.

"I'm afraid it's a touch of bronchitis," he told her. "I'll write out a prescription for you but I would also strongly recommend that you wear some knickers. It won't help your illness, not wearing them."

She looked at him quizzically.

"Are you trying to tell me that just by looking down my throat you could see I wasn't wearing any knickers?"

"Well . . . er . . . yes," he answered.

"In that case," she said, "would you mind looking up my a**e and telling me if my hat's on straight?"

Why are men who have pierced ears ready for marriage?
They've known pain and bought jewellery.

A journalist interviewed a local woman when he heard she'd had four children, all born three years apart on May 20th.

"That's astonishing," he remarked, "and what does your husband do for a living?"

"Oh, he's a precision grinder," came the reply.

As John got undressed, ready for bed, his wife turned to him in alarm.

"John, why have you got that cork sticking out of your bum?"

"Oh no," groaned John, putting his head in his hands."If only I hadn't gone to the tip this morning," he continued.

"While I was there, I spotted this bottle glinting in the sun. I rubbed off the mud to get a good look and a genie appeared. He said he'd grant me anything I wanted."

"Well, what did you say?" asked his wife impatiently.

"I said, 'No sh*t!'"

Over a few pints of beer at the local, two men were so engrossed in conversation that they didn't notice the time. Suddenly last orders were called and the first man cursed out loud.

"Bugger! That's me for the cold-shoulder treatment, I promised the wife I'd be home early."

He looked glumly into his pint and continued, "I just can't win. Whenever I go out I make sure none of the doors squeak, I oil the garden gate, I move anything I might trip over in the dark and then when I get home, I take my shoes off before going upstairs, undress in the bathroom and slip very quietly into bed in the pitch black. And it never bloody works! She still turns over and shouts, 'Where have you been until this time of night?'"

"No, mate," said the second man, "you're doing it all wrong. When I get home late at night, I swing the garden gate backwards and forwards to make as much squeaking noise as possible. Then I slam the front door, turn on all the lights, and stomp up the stairs into the bedroom. I jump into bed and give the wife a good nudge in the ribs and say, 'How about it, then, love?' and you can bet you've never seen a woman sleep so deeply."

"It's no good!" cried the downtrodden husband. "I can't go on. I'm off to join the Foreign Legion."

"Very well," retorted the wife, "but don't let me find you trailing sand all over my nice new carpet when you get back."

A man walked into his home and yelled at his wife.
"Mildred, I've just discovered our marriage is illegal!"
"How come?" she replied.
"Your father didn't have a licence for that shotgun."

"Look at this!" exclaimed the angry husband to his wife. "The bank has returned the cheque you wrote last week."

"Oh, great," she replied. "I wonder what I'll spend it on next."

BRIEF ENCOUNTERS

I went to this discussion group on premature ejaculation.
In fact, I was five minutes early, but it was all over.

☞ ★ ☜

There's one thing wrong with oral sex – the view.

☞ ★ ☜

What do you get if you merge Xerox with Wurlitzer?
A company that makes reproductive organs.

☞ ★ ☜

Words of wisdom from a philosopher: "It all comes down to the same thing in the end. Live life like a dog. If you can't eat it or f*ck it, then p*ss on it."

An ornithological meteorologist is a man who looks at birds and can tell whether . . .

Did you hear about the unhappy atheist?
He had no one to talk to during orgasm.

'Don't be deceived by Dennis.
He's a titan in bed.'

ANIMAL ALERT!

A man took his dog to the vet's and asked for its tail to be completely removed.
"But why?" asked the vet. "That's a bit drastic."
The man replied, "My mother-in-law's coming to stay next week and I want to make sure there are no signs of welcome."

As the stranger walked into the store, he saw a sign that read 'Beware of the dog'. The next moment he saw an old sheepdog sprawled out on the floor, fast asleep.
"Is that the dog referred to on the sign?" he asked the storekeeper.
"Yes, it surely is," came the reply.
"Well, it's hard to believe the dog is so dangerous. Why did you put the sign up?"
"Because since I've put the sign up, people have stopped tripping over him."

A man goes into the vet's.
"Say, 'Aaah . . . ' " says the vet.
"Why?" asks the man.
"Because your dog's just died."

'Don't worry, it's an old sign.'

Three young women are at a cocktail party. The conversation turns to their husbands.

The first woman, smiling smugly, says, "My husband is taking me on a romantic break to the French Riviera for two weeks."

The second boasts, "Well, my husband has just bought me a brand new Porsche."

The third shrugs and says, "Well, to be perfectly honest with you, ladies, we don't have much money or many material possessions. However, one thing I can tell you about my husband is that thirteen canaries can stand shoulder to shoulder on his erect penis."

After this, the first woman looks ashamed. "Girls, I've got a confession to make. I was only trying to impress you. You know that holiday I was telling you about? Well, it's not to the French Riviera, it's to my parents' house for two weeks."

The second one says, "Oh, I'm just as bad. It's not a Porsche he bought me, but an old, battered Skoda."

"Well, I also have a confession to make," said the third. "Canary number thirteen has to stand on one leg."

Why do dogs stick their snouts in blondes' crotches? Because they can.

What do you do if a pit bull terrier tries to mount your leg?
Fake an orgasm.

A man tried to smuggle a puppy into the country to avoid the quarantine laws, but accidentally drew attention to himself walking through customs. He had put the dog down his trousers, but every time he took a step, his whole body would shake and he kept making little moaning sounds.

"Excuse me, sir, is there anything wrong?" enquired the customs official.

"Yes, officer," gasped the man in a strangled voice. "I tried to smuggle a puppy into the country by putting it down my trousers."

"Oh, yes?" smiled the officer knowingly. "You've just discovered it's not house-trained, have you?"

"No," replied the agitated man, "I've just discovered it's not weaned."

Three friends are sitting round the fire talking about their dogs. The first one tells them his dog is called Woodman.

"Let me show you why. Woodman – go, boy."

At that, the dog takes a log from the side of the fire and carves a beautiful statue of a bird. Then the second demonstrates why his dog is called Stoneman.

"Go, boy, go." Immediately the dog jumps up, takes part of the stonework from the fire and trims it into a carving of an Indian.

Finally, the third friend says, "My dog's called Ironman. Watch this." The man heats the fire tongs until they are blisteringly hot and then tells his mates, "I'll touch him on the balls with these and you watch him make a bolt for the door."

A man goes into a bar with a giraffe and they both get horribly drunk until the giraffe collapses in a dead faint on the floor. The man gets up to leave. "Hey!" says the bartender. "You can't leave that lyin' there." "It's not a lion, it's a giraffe," says the man.

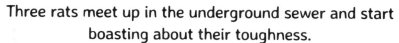

Three rats meet up in the underground sewer and start boasting about their toughness.

"I'm not scared of anything," says the first. "I'll raid any house, take whatever I want and they never catch me."

"That's nothing," replies the second scornfully. "Whenever I see rat poison I just chew it up and spit it out." They wait for the third to speak, but he gets up and starts to move away.

"Hey, what's up, where are you going?"

He replies haughtily, "I ain't got time for this. I'm off to f*ck the cat."

Two ducks meet in the hotel bar, have a few drinks and decide to book into a room for the night. But ever mindful of safe sex, they ask room service for a packet of condoms. A few minutes later the condoms arrive and the waiter asks the male duck, "Shall I put it on your bill, sir?"

"Certainly not!" snaps the duck. "What do you think I am, some sort of pervert?"

A man walked into a club with a pet snake under his arm.

"Hey, you can't bring that snake in here – he might bite one of our members," said the manager.

"Oh, that's no problem, you just get a friend to suck the poison out."

"But what if he bites someone up the backside?"

"Well, then you really find out who your friends are."

A man went to the pet shop to buy a parrot but the only one on offer cost £500.

"Why is it so expensive?" he asked.

"Ah, well, it's a very special parrot – it lays square eggs," said the pet shop owner.

"How very odd. OK, I'll take it, but just one thing – does it talk?"

"Well, it can, but up till now all I've heard is 'Aaagh, oooh, bugger . . . '"

A woman was given a parrot for her birthday, but the bird had grown up with a bad attitude and some of the foulest language she had ever heard.

Try as she might – teaching it new words, soothing it with music – she could not get the parrot to change. One day, he was even worse than usual. The woman got so angry that she put him in the freezer and closed the door. The bird could be heard squawking, kicking and screaming, and then all went quiet. Frightened that she may have harmed him, she quickly opened the door and the parrot calmly stepped out.

"If I've offended you in any way, I'm very sorry," he said. "I promise it will never happen again. By the way, what did the chicken do?"

A woman was walking through the park when she spotted a man and a dog playing chess. She watched the game for a few minutes, then remarked, "I can't believe what I'm seeing. A dog playing chess. What a clever animal!"
"He's not that clever, madam," replied the man. "I've beaten him four games out of six."

A man buys two dogs from the pet shop and no matter what he does he can't stop them from sh*gging each other. He tries throwing cold water over them, putting pepper on their backsides and then changing their diet, but nothing works. In desperation, he rings the vet in the middle of the night to tell him the problem.
"Here's a good idea," says the vet. "Why don't you take the telephone over to the dogs and give each of them a ring?"
"Will that really work?" replies the astonished man.
"Well, it damned well worked for me!" says the vet, slamming down the phone.

'We'd better do as he says.'

"Hey, does your dog bite?" asks the man sitting down next to a guy with a dog at his feet.

"No," he replies. But a moment later, the dog lurches forward and takes an almighty bite out of the man's ankle.

"Hey, I thought you said your dog didn't bite!" he says angrily.

"That's right," says the dog owner, "that there's not my dog."

Before the race meeting had begun, some of the horses were boasting about their achievements.

"Well, I've won over half the races I've been in, and I've been placed in the rest," said the bay horse.

"I've won 18 races out of 24," said the black.

"I've only lost one race in the whole of my career," said the white.

"Excuse me," interrupted a greyhound who'd been listening to them,

"I've won 20 races out of 20."

The horses looked down on him in astonishment.

"Bloody hell," said one, "a talking dog!"

TALL TALES

How did Pinocchio find out he
was made of wood?
His hand caught fire.

Snow White was asked to leave Fairyland last week.
She was found sitting on Pinocchio's face saying,
"Tell a lie, tell the truth, tell a lie, tell the truth . . . "

This is the story of the three bears.
One of them married a giraffe.
The other two put him up to it.

Did you hear about the cowboy who arrived in town
wearing a paper shirt, paper trousers, a paper hat and
paper boots?
The sherriff arrested him for rustling.

While on holiday, the Seven Dwarfs visit the local convent to buy some souvenirs.

They meet up with the Mother Superior and Dopey stops to talk to her.

"Excuse me, your holy one, do you have any short nuns here?"

Mother Superior is puzzled by the question, but replies, "Not very short, maybe one or two around 5 ft."

"Are you sure there aren't any nuns about 3 ft in height?" he persists.

"No, no, no one like that."

As the dwarfs leave, the Mother Superior follows them quietly down the road to try to discover the reason for such an odd question. She overhears the other dwarfs asking Dopey what was said, and he replies, "She said they don't have any."

On hearing this, the dwarfs fall about laughing and chanting, "Dopey's f*cked a penguin, Dopey's f*cked a penguin!"

ZOO TIME

The elephant keeper at the zoo was grooming his animal when a man stopped to ask him the time. The keeper got down on his knees, swung the elephant's balls to and fro and replied, "Half-past four."

Amazed, the man caught up with his friends and urged them to return with him to see this extraordinary occurrence. They agreed and all went back to the keeper.

"Excuse me, do you know the time, please?" said one of the friends.

Again the man got on his knees, gently handled the elephant's balls and replied, "Four forty-five."

After the party moved on, the first man's curiosity got the better of him and he returned to the keeper.

"I'll give you £50 if you show me how you can tell the time."

"If you insist," said the keeper. He beckoned the man to get down on his knees as well, then moved the elephant's balls to one side and said, "You see that clock tower over there?"

A gorilla has escaped from the local zoo and taken refuge at the top of a tree in a neighbouring garden. The householder rings the zookeeper who arrives ten minutes later with a pair of handcuffs, a Doberman pinscher, a stick and a shotgun.

"OK," says the zookeeper to the man. "I'm going to go up after him and poke him with this sharp stick. When he falls to the ground, the dog will go for his balls. As the gorilla puts his hands over them to protect himself, you slip on the handcuffs."

"That sounds easy enough," replies the man, "but what's the shotgun for?"

"Now listen carefully, this is most important. If I fall out of the tree before the gorilla – shoot the f*cking dog!"

COUNTRY MATTERS

A man who had done a lot for his village was complaining about the lack of respect he received from the rest of the inhabitants.

"For instance," he said, "see all those beautifully mown lawns, the abundance of flowers, the avenue of trees? I did all that, but do they call me John the Horticulturist? No, they bloody don't! And look at the stunning new village hall and the church wall. I did all that but do they call me John the Builder? Not bloody likely!

I sh*g one sheep . . . "

Backing out of the farmyard on his milk float, the milkman ran over and killed the prize rooster. Feeling very bad about it, he sought out the farmer's wife to tell her the bad news.

"Excuse me, madam, I'm so sorry but I've run over your

prize rooster and I would like to replace it."
"Well, that's fine with me," she said. "You'll find the
chickens behind the barn."

*A local girl is walking in the country when
she spies two brothers harvesting wheat.
"Hi, boys, why don't you take a break from
work and we can have a good time. You'll
have to wear these condoms because I
don't want to get pregnant."
Entranced, the boys immediately agree.
A year goes by. One day one of the
brothers says, "Our Jack, do you remember
the time we met that girl in the cornfield?"
"I do that," Jack replies dreamily.
"Well, do you care if she gets pregnant?"
"No, not anymore."
"Nor me. Let's take these things off now.""*

Two chickens were standing at the side of the road.
One said to the other, "For goodness sake, don't cross
that road, or everyone will want to know why."

As the man parks his Rolls-Royce in the village car park, one of the locals comes up to him and says admiringly, "That's a lovely car you have there. How much did it cost?"

"About £200,000."

"Blimey, how much petrol does it take?"

"29 gallons."

"And how many miles does it do to the gallon?"

"About two miles. I work for Cunard, you know."

"Well, I work f*cking hard as well," the man retorts, "but I still can't afford a Rolls-Royce!"

Two shepherds are driving a lorry full of sheep back to their farm when suddenly the brakes fail as they come hurtling towards a sharp bend in the road.

"Quick!" shouts one of the men. "Jump for it."

"What about the sheep?" shouts the other.

"Oh, f*ck the sheep!" yells the first shepherd.

"What!" cries the second, "do you think we have time?"

The farm inspector was on his annual tour of the county and had arrived at Farmer Giles' place.
"So how many sheep do you have?" the inspector asked.
"I don't know," replied the farmer.
"Every time I try to count them, I fall asleep."

'Your dog's worrying my sheep.'

A kindly man came across a young boy whose cart had shed its load of manure.

"Come back with me," he said, "we'll get you cleaned up, have a spot of lunch, then I'll bring back my two sons to help you clear the road."

The boy hesitated. "I'm not sure," he faltered, "my dad might not like that."

"I think your dad will be pleased you're doing something about it," said the man and eventually the boy was persuaded.

A couple of hours later, they returned with his two sons to begin clearing the load.

"By the way, where is your dad?" asked the man.

"Under the manure," came the reply.

"Don't worry about the cow," said the vet to the farmer. "It just needs a pessary. Take this tube, simply insert it in the cow's bum and blow."

When the farmer returned to his farm, he explained the method to his cowman and left him to it. Half an hour later, the cowman came looking for him.

"Sorry, Mr Brooks, I can't seem to blow the damn thing up."

Farmer Brooks went back to the cow shed, took the tube out, turned it round and re-inserted it. He then blew the pessary up first time.
"Why did you turn the tube round?" asked the cowman.
"Well, I'm not sucking the end that's been in your mouth!"

A local crop dealer is on his way to visit a farm out in the middle of nowhere. It's a long distance to travel, so he puts his foot down and is going at 60mph when he's passed by a three-legged chicken that soon disappears into the distance. The dealer gets to the farm and carries out his business. Then he remembers the chicken and asks the farmer about it.

"Oh, yes, that's one of our three-legged chickens. We raised them ourselves. You see, there's me, my wife and our John, and we all like the legs, but it was a waste when we had to kill two chickens for our Sunday lunch."

"And are they tasty?" asked the crop dealer.

"I don't know, we haven't caught one of the buggers yet!"

Towards the end of market day, a vet approached one of the old farmers.
"Have you ever considered artificial insemination for your herd of cows, Mr Woodall?"
"No, thanks, I'll stick to the old-fashioned way if it's all the same to you."
"OK, but if you change your mind, give us a ring and we'll take it from there."
On the way home, the farmer pondered the vet's words, but couldn't imagine how a cow could be serviced without a bull.
His curiosity eventually got the better of him. He rang the vet and asked for his cow to be serviced as soon as possible.
"OK," replied the vet. "If you can get a few things prepared. Wash the cow's backside, put down some clean straw and have a bucket of hot water and a stool ready."
When all was ready, the vet arrived.
"Have you done everything I asked?"
"That I have," replied the farmer. "I've even hammered a nail in the door for you to hang your trousers on."

"That bloody bull's going to the knacker's yard!" yelled the farmer.
"It's nearly killed me three times."
"Oh, give him one more chance," replied his wife."

A ventriloquist was being shown around a farm by a local yokel.
As a joke, the ventriloquist made the bull look as though he was saying, "Hello, there."
The yokel did not react. So then the ventriloquist made the hen say, "This man has been stealing all my eggs."
At this point the yokel got very flustered and said, "When we get to the sow, don't believe a word she says!"

What can cows do that women can't?
Stand up to their t*ts in water without getting their fannies wet.

PARK LIFE

A Scotsman, on the way home from a heavy drinking
session with his mates, collapses on to a park bench
and falls into a very deep stupor. Some time later, two
girls walk past and, on seeing him, debate whether he
has anything under his kilt.

They decide to look and discover he's stark naked.
"We really ought to leave him a record of our visit," one
says to the other, so, giggling with delight, they tie a
blue ribbon round his willy before moving on.

Finally the Scotsman comes round and, bursting for a
pee, staggers behind a bush. When he sees the ribbon
he smiles and says to it, "I don't know where you've
been, or what you've been up to, but I see you've won
first prize!"

*It was so cold in the park last month
that the local flasher was reported to
be describing himself to the women
he met.*

In the park one day, man walked up to a policeman with a tiger trailing behind him.

"Excuse me, officer," he said. "I found this tiger earlier today, and now he just keeps following me around. What should I do with him?"

"Hmm," said the policeman, "I think you should take him to the zoo."

The man agreed that this was a good idea, and off he went with the tiger in tow.

Next day, the policeman was walking his beat again when he saw the same man, who still had the tiger with him.

"Here," said the policeman. "I thought I told you to take that tiger to the zoo?"

"I did," said the man, "and we had a great time. Now we're going bowling, and tonight we're off to the cinema."

A man came staggering through the park well and truly p*ssed when he saw a man doing press-ups. After watching him for a minute, the drunk started to laugh.

"What's so funny?" asked the man angrily.

"I think you ought to know your woman's left you," replied the drunk.

SHIPWRECKED!

A man is abandoned on a desert island. After six years, a beautiful shapely blonde in a wet-suit gets washed ashore, and they get into conversation.

"How long have you been here?" she asks.

"Six years," he says.

"That's a long time. Would you like a drink?"

"I'd love one," replies the castaway eagerly.

With that she unzips a pocket in her wet suit and gets out a bottle of Scotch. The blonde then asks if he would like a cigarette.

"Yes, please!" he replies, so she unzips another pocket to produce a packet of cigarettes and a lighter.

"How long did you say you'd been here?" she asks again.

"Six years."

"Ah . . . then would you like to play around?"

The castaway is astonished. "Don't tell me you've got a set of golf clubs in there as well!"

A man was stranded on a desert island and one day found a bottle washed up on the beach. Inside the bottle was

a genie who was so grateful for being let out that he said he would grant the man one wish. After some thought, the man said he had always wanted to visit the Far East, so he asked if the genie could build a road from the island to the Great Wall of China.

"My goodness," replied the genie. "I'm not sure I can do that. Imagine all the work that would be involved in building across oceans and mountainous landscapes, all the materials. . . . No, I don't think that's such a good idea."

"OK," said the man. He thought for a moment and said, "Another thing I've always wanted is to understand women. I want to know what makes them laugh, why they get so angry, why they cry . . . "

"About this road," said the genie, "do you want a motorway or will a dual carriageway do you?"

A man had been stranded on a desert island for two years when he experienced severe shaking of the ground and noticed a great tidal wave bearing down upon him. "Oh Lord, please help me," he prayed. Suddenly, a boat appeared and a man aboard shouted to him urgently,

"Quick, get on board, before the tidal wave comes!"
"No, no, I have faith in Jesus," said the castaway. A few moments passed and another boat appeared.

"Quick, man, don't be silly, get on board, there's not much time left."

"No, thank you, I have faith in Jesus."
With only seconds to go, another boat appeared and a voice called out in panic, "If you don't get over here right this minute, it'll be too late!"

"No, thank you. I have faith in Jesus."
The next moment, the tidal wave hit the island, smashing everything to pieces. The poor castaway drowned. Later, in heaven, the man met Jesus and said reproachfully, "I had faith in you. I can't believe this has happened."

"What do you mean, you can't believe it?" cried Jesus.
"I sent three bloody boats, didn't I?"

After two months of being shipwrecked on a desert island, the man sees a barrel floating towards the shore. Holding on to the barrel is a stunningly beautiful naked woman. As he rushes down to meet her she says, "I think I have something you want."

The man's eyes light up. "I don't believe it!" he gasps. "You've got beer in that barrel?"

A bloke found himself stranded on a desert island with six women. To keep it fair, it was decided he would service a different woman every night and have Mondays free. After a few months, the man was exhausted from performing constantly every night except one.

One day, to his joy, he found washed up on the beach a man who would be able to take some of the workload from him. But his hopes were shattered when the man's first words were, "Hi, gorgeous, how about the kiss of life?"

"Oh f*ck," thought the man, "there goes Mondays."

SKID ROW

An old tramp walks into social services with a pig on a lead. "Can you find somewhere for me and my pig to live?" he asks. "Just a bed if that's all you've got. My pig can sleep underneath it."
"But what about the smell?" asks the official.
"Oh, the pig don't mind."

The down-and-out man had spent his morning begging from street to street. He hadn't done very well and was just about to give up when he noticed a very posh woman walking up the private road to her mansion.
"Excuse me, madam," he said as politely as possible. "Can you spare a bob or two?"
"I'll do better than that," she said. "How are you with a paint brush?"
"Erm, OK, I suppose," he replied, puzzled.
"Good, there's a can of orange paint

here. If you paint the porch round the
back, then I'll pay you a decent
day's wages."
The tramp disappeared and nothing was
seen of him for the next three hours
when he reappeared with an empty can.
"All finished?" she asked.
"It is," he replied, "but just one thing,"
he added helpfully.
"It's a Ferrari round the back, not
a Porsche."

'Yes, it's a pretty rough area. . . . Morning, vicar.'

BAD MANNERS

A dirty old man picked up a beautiful young girl in the local pub and invited her out for dinner. To his surprise she accepted, and they went off to the poshest restaurant in town where she ordered all the most expensive food and drink on the menu. Astonished, the man asked her if she always had such a big appetite. "Only when someone wants to get into my knickers," she replied.

Ever since the new cook had arrived at camp, he had been treated miserably. They'd thrown away his clothes, turned his bed upside down and hidden his post. Eventually, however, they grew bored and told him there would be no more tricks.
"You really mean that?" he said.
"Yes," they assured him.
"OK, good, then I'll stop p*ssing in the soup."

Three men are discussing what to buy their wives for their birthdays.

"I'm going to get my wife some sexy underwear and a pair of Italian shoes, then if she doesn't like one, hopefully she'll like the other."

"That's a good idea," says the second man. "I'll get my wife two presents as well and maybe one of them will be alright.

Let's see – I think I'll get her a gold necklace and a swanky evening dress."

"What about you, Jack?" they say, turning to the third man who has remained morosely quiet.

"Oh, I know what I'm getting Doreen, a mink coat and a dildo.

If she doesn't like the coat, she can go f*ck herself."

Why do Australian men come so quickly?
Because they can't wait to get down the pub to tell their mates.

Why do Scotsmen wear kilts?
So the sheep won't hear the zip.

A miserly old woman was always trying to find ways of saving money and came upon the idea of feeding her husband cheap dog food. It took a few days for him to get used to it, but when she insisted it was the best minced steak he had no reason to be suspicious. Three months went by. One afternoon she received a phone call from the local hospital to say her husband had had an accident. She rushed to casualty and asked the doctor on duty what had happened.

"Just a few broken bones, really. An odd accident, though. It seems he was hit by a car when he suddenly sat down in the middle of the road and tried to lick his backside."

"I'm really fed up with my wife's slovenly ways," complained Bob. "This morning, I went to p*ss in the sink and it was full of dishes!"

How can you tell if a woman is wearing pantyhose? When she farts her ankles swell up.

'Thanks . . . I don't normally accept drinks off
ugly men, but I'm skint.'

**"You will still love me now we're married,
won't you?" asked the newly-wed girl.
"Even more," he replied. "I've a thing
about married women."**

"But if I give you oral sex, won't you lose respect
for me?"
"Not if you're good at it." he replied.

GOING OUT

Three sisters, named Flora, Fiona and Fanny lived in the same village in Yorkshire and were renowned for their beauty, although all of them had extra-large feet. One evening, Flora and Fiona went to the local bop and soon found themselves chatting to some lads from the next village.

"By gum," said one of the lads. "Haven't you got big feet!"

"Oh, that's nowt," they replied. "You should see our Fanny's."

The lift was packed solid with people as the doors closed. The attendant called out, "Which floors please?"

A man standing at the back shouted out, "Ballroom!" and a lady in front of him cried, "Oh, I'm so sorry, I didn't know I was crushing you that much."

On her way home from an all-night party, the girl was stopped by the traffic cops and breathalyzed. Looking at the results one of the policemen said, "You've had a few stiff ones tonight, Miss."
"That's amazing," she said. "I didn't know you could tell that as well."

'What girl in the cake?'

WOT LARKS!

What do you you call a group of twelve men with
large willies?
A hung jury.

*"Come on, girl," whispered the boastful
man to the beautiful girl after a few
drinks. "How about coming back to my
place and letting me give you
six inches?"*
*"No, thanks," she replied. "I don't think
you've got the energy to get it up
three times."*

A husband and wife are admiring their
newborn son.
"My goodness, just look at the size of his willy," says
dad, proudly. "Yes, sweetheart," answers his wife, "but
at least he's got
your nose."

As she left the room, the sweet young girl said to her boss, "Oh, just one more thing, Mr Arno, you've left the barrack doors open."

It wasn't until later he understood what she meant when he looked down and realized he'd left his flies undone. He pressed the intercom and said, "Maureen, can you come in here for a moment please?"

As she walked in, he said proudly, "When I left the barrack doors open this morning, did you see a soldier standing to attention?"

"Oh, no," she replied sweetly. "I saw a shell-shocked veteran who'd seen better days."

What do you call a man with a 4-inch penis?
Norm.

A man goes to the doctor's because his penis is a massive 60 inches long.

"It's ruining my life," complains the man. "Is there anything you can do?"

"I'm sorry, there isn't," says the doctor, "but I think I have an answer to your problem. I've heard there's a deep pond in the middle of Crossways Wood. When you find it, you will see a frog sitting on a lily pad. You must ask the frog to marry you and when it says no, your penis will shorten by ten inches."

However absurd the story, the man is so desperate that he sets out for the wood. Sure enough, there's a frog sitting on the lily pad.

"Hey, frog," the man shouts, "will you marry me?"

"No," replies the frog, and the man's penis shrinks by ten inches.

The man is overcome with happiness. Two more times he asks the frog to marry him and the man's penis shrinks another 20 inches.

Wonderful, thinks the man, just once more and it'll be perfect.

"Hey, froggy, will you marry me?"

By this time the frog is so annoyed with all the pestering that he shouts back in irritation. "I'm fed up with telling you – no, no and no again!"

A male visitor to a country club ends up in the female locker room by mistake. He is unaware of this until halfway through his shower, when two ladies come in and he hears them talking. In panic, all he can think of is to escape without being recognized. He wraps a towel round his face and runs naked from the room.

"My goodness," exclaims the first woman. "That certainly wasn't my husband."

"Nor mine," says the second.

"In fact," continues the first, "he's not even a member of this club."

An arrogant man asks his wife if she would like some ice-cream he's brought back from the supermarket.
"How hard is it?" she asks.
"About as hard as my d*ck," he brags.
"OK, pour me some then."

GIRL TALK

Two ladies are talking in the laundrette:
"Has your husband been circumcised?" says one.
"No," replies the other. "He's always been a
complete d*ck."

Two women talking:
"How do you keep your youth?" says
the first.
"I lock him in the cupboard," replies
the second.

Two girls are walking along the promenade when
a holiday photographer steps forward.
"Hold on, Jean, he's going to focus."
"What! Both at the same time?"

Two women are chatting on a bus.
"I've got a dreadful sore throat,"
says one.
"Oh you poor thing! When I've got a
sore throat I suck on a Life Saver."
"Ah, that's easy for you. You live near
the seaside."

"Oh, Patsy, you know that gorgeous man across the road? He was banging on my door for almost an hour last night."
"Well, why didn't you open it?"
"I didn't want to let him out."

A woman said to her friend, "Do you
smoke after sex?"
"Gosh, I've never looked," she replied.

A bad football team is like an old bra.
No cups and very little support.

OFFICE POLITICS

His secretary was absolutely terrible.
"Why don't you answer the bloody phone?" he said
in exasperation.
"Because I'm damned well fed-up," she replied. "Nine
times out of ten it's for you!"

*The ambitious PA went out for dinner
with her boss and when the bill
arrived she said, "I must insist we go
Dutch. You pay for dinner and
the rest of the evening will be on me."*

"You can use my Dictaphone," said the office Casanova
to the new secretary.
"No, thanks. I'll use my finger, if it's all the same with
you," she replied.

The interview for secretary had been going well until the boss asked, "How good are you on the typewriter?" "Pretty good," she replied, "but I'm better on the floor."

Jack and his colleagues were off on their annual sales conference. Relaxing in the bar afterwards, they began recounting their most embarrassing moments.
"What about you, Colin?" asked Jack.
Colin hesitated and then said, "I suppose it was when my mother came into my room and found me playing with myself."
"Well, that's nothing to worry about. Young boys often do that sort of thing," said Jack, somewhat disappointed.
"Yes, I know," replied Colin, "but this was only last week."

The young girl arrived for an interview to become a trainee executive. "So, Miss Brightly, what are your qualifications?"

"Well I graduated from Oxford with a first-class honours degree, having achieved the highest marks ever. I then spent a year in the States, running the day-to-day business of a small airline and in my spare time wrote a textbook on modern business practices."

"Well, that's wonderful," enthused the interview panel. "Is there anything you wish to add?"

"Yes, I'm a pathological liar."

After the job interview, the post was given to a voluptuous young girl.

"You'll be expected to do the same things here as you did in your last job," said her new boss.

"Oh, that's fine by me," she replied, "as long as I can kneel on something soft."

It was the young girl's first day in her new job as PA to the company

director. *Before she was called in to his room, one of the other secretaries took her aside.*

"I think I ought to warn you that your new boss is a right randy old devil. He'll rip your dress off at the first opportunity."

"Thanks for warning me," replied the girl. "I'll remember to wear an old dress in future."

'Congratulations on your promotion.
It's a creeper.'

"Excuse me, sir, may I have tomorrow afternoon off?
The wife wants me to go shopping with her."
"Certainly not."
"Thank you, sir, I knew you'd understand."

The local bank was held up by four masked gunmen, and customers and staff were ordered to lie face down on the floor.
Everyone did as they were told except one young girl who lay down on her back.
"Don't be silly, this is a bank robbery, not the office party," whispered her friend. "Lie down the other way."

A man rings up his boss to tell him he won't be
in to work.
"I'm sorry, I'm sick," he tells him.
"Sick again," says the boss angrily. "This seems to be
happening a lot. How sick are you?"
"Pretty sick," replies the man. "I'm in bed with my sister."

The morning after the office party, the husband put his head in his hands and groaned loudly.

"Oh, bloody hell, what a party last night, I can't remember a thing about it. Did I make a prat of myself?"

"You sure did," replied his wife. "You put your hand up the skirt of your boss's wife and told your boss to p*ss off."

"Sh*t! What happened?"

'Stop whingeing, Wilson, we all have to start somewhere.'

"He sacked you."
"Well f*ck him, the b*stard."
"I did," replied the wife, "and you've got
your job back."

The company was losing money and the boss had no other option but to get rid of one of his staff – either Jack or Beryl.

He decides to tell them straight away and spots Beryl putting on her coat ready for going home.

"Hello, Beryl," he says hesitantly, "there's something I've got to tell you. I need to lay you or Jack off."

"Then jack off," she replied angrily. "I've got a headache!"

The ambitious city type lived for his job, nothing else mattered. Every evening and all weekend he would bring papers home to work on. One day he left some important papers at home and, in a panic, rushed back to get them. As he was passing the spare room, he caught sight of his wife and his boss in bed together.

Later that day he mentioned what he had seen to a colleague.
"Why, that's appalling, are you going back tomorrow to try and catch them at it?"
"Good gracious, no! It was lucky he didn't see me this time."

Three dentists and three bankers find themselves together at the railway ticket office. The dentists each buy a ticket but the bankers buy one between them.
"How are you all going to travel on one ticket?" ask the dentists.

"You'll see," the bankers reply.

The dentists take their seats on the train, but the bankers all cram into the toilet. The conductor appears, shouting "Tickets please!". He knocks on the toilet door and a ticket is passed to him. The dentists are impressed and decide to do the same on the return journey. They buy one ticket, but to their amazement the bankers don't buy a ticket at all.

They all get on the train, the three dentists crammed in one toilet, the three bankers in another.

A few minutes later, one of the bankers leaves his toilet, knocks on the other toilet door and shouts, "Tickets please!"

SERVICE SECTOR

Bill, the local barber, had a secret remedy to restore hair and on the odd occasion he would pass it on to his very special customers.

One such customer came in and asked Bill to give him the remedy for £1,000. After some thought, Bill agreed and told him that all he needed to do to restore hair to his bald patch was apply some female secretions.

"But how do I know it works?" replied the customer. "You've still got a bald patch on your head."

"Maybe," said Bill. "But have you ever seen a better moustache?"

An ageing, out-of-work actor received a phone call from his agent telling him to be in Leeds the following Friday for a part in the Christmas panto. The actor was thrilled. At last, he would be treading the boards once again!

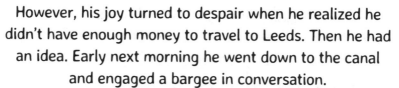

However, his joy turned to despair when he realized he didn't have enough money to travel to Leeds. Then he had an idea. Early next morning he went down to the canal and engaged a bargee in conversation.

"Excuse me, bargee," he said. "I am to appear in a pantomime at Leeds Theatre next Friday and I wondered if anyone was going my way?"

"As it happens, I am," replied the bargee. "I set off at six o'clock in the morning, and we'll make it by Thursday as long as we get through the locks without a mishap."

True to his word, the bargee set off at six the next morning with the ageing actor on board. As the first lock came into view, the lock keeper shouted down, "Hello there, what are you carrying?"

"I'm carrying 10 ton of pig sh*te and the actor Cyril Carstairs," replied the bargee.

At the second lock, the lock keeper asked the same question and again he got the same reply.

"I'm carrying 10 ton of pig sh*te and the actor Cyril Carstairs."

So the journey continued until they came to the outskirts of Leeds and the final, 22nd lock. As they approached, the actor tapped the bargee on the shoulder.

"Excuse me, bargee," he said. "We're coming to the final lock, and I wonder, just this once, if I could have top billing?"

It was Saturday morning and the newspaper man was collecting the week's money. When he got to 74 Prospect Road he rang the bell, but got no answer. Just as he was about to leave, he suddenly had a feeling that someone was standing just behind the door. He put his ear to the wood and could hear a great deal of panting and gasping. "It's the newspaper man," he called. A voice was heard from the other side, "Can you come back in ten minutes? I'm just paying the milk bill."

A couple moved into a new house, close to a busy main road.

Unfortunately, every time a bus trundled by, the wardrobe door flew open. The woman rang a local carpenter who said he'd come round that afternoon to fix it. He inspected the door closely, but could find nothing wrong.

"I'll just have a look inside," he said, but as he stepped through the door the woman's husband walked into the bedroom.

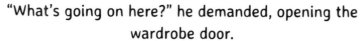

"What's going on here?" he demanded, opening the wardrobe door.

"You'll never believe this," said the carpenter sheepishly. "But I'm waiting for a bus."

Johnny was looking for his mate Bob Cox and thought he might be having his hair cut. He popped his head round the barber shop door and called out, "Bob Cox in here?"

"Sorry, no," replied the barber, "we only do shaves and haircuts."

'I sometimes wish you had another job.'

The simpleton's car broke down and the garage man arrived to take a look at it.

"Oh, yeah, sh*t in the carburettor," said the mechanic.

"Really?" asks the simpleton. "How often will I have to do that?"

The milkman delivers the milk the day before Christmas and rings the bell of number 11, hoping for a festive tip. The door opens to reveal a beautiful woman wearing a see-through nightie. She takes the milkman by the hand and guides him upstairs where she makes mad, passionate love to him. Afterwards, they return downstairs where she cooks a delicious fried breakfast and hands him £1.

"I don't understand," says the puzzled milkman. "What's going on?"

*She replies, "When I asked my husband whether I should give you a £5 tip, he replied, 'F*ck the milkman, give him £1.' The breakfast was my idea."*

The young man was selling encyclopedias from door to door. He had one set left as he knocked at the cottage door and a voice called out, "Hello?"

"I'm selling the latest, most up-to-date encyclopedias," the man called back.

The door opened to reveal a voluptuous woman.

"Well, hello," she said sexily.

All of a sudden, the man burst into floods of tears.

"What's wrong?" she asked, alarmed at his behaviour.

"I've had a terrible week," he sobbed. "My wife left me on Monday, the house burned down Tuesday, yesterday someone stole my car and now today I'm going to be f*cked out of my last set of encyclopedias."

A man walked into a barber's shop. "Can you part my hair from ear to ear?" he asked.

The barber did what was asked.

But that afternoon the man came back. "What's wrong?" asked the barber. "Are you tired of the style already?"

"No," the man replied angrily, "I'm just fed up with everybody whispering in my nose."

TAKE A PEW

It was Saturday night and Ted and his two mates were all dressed up, ready to paint the town red. But first, as usual, Ted popped into church for confession. "Forgive me, Father, for I have sinned. I slept with a woman who was not my wife."

"I suppose it was Christina from the dairy?"

"No, Father."

"Don't tell me it was Stacey at the Kings Arms?"

"No, Father."

"Then it must have been that brazen hussy Marie from the newsagent's?"

After the priest had given out the penance, Ted went back outside to meet his friends. He smiled at them saying, "It's worked again, lads – I've got the names of another three ravers!"

The young priest was about to hear his first confession. The old priest sat to one side to keep an eye on him. When it was over, the young priest asked how he had done.

"Not too bad," replied the old priest. "But in future a bit less 'Really!', 'Never!', 'Cor!', and 'Wow!' and a bit more tut-tutting might be better idea."

'Did I hear you say this was your first christening?'

A vicar went into a pet shop looking for a nice pet to keep him company while he wrote his sermons.

"I've got just what you need," said the pet shop owner. "Take a look at this parrot. Not only does he talk, but if you pull the string on his left leg he'll sing 'Rock of Ages' and if you pull the string on his right leg, he'll recite the Lord's Prayer."

"That is truly remarkable!" exclaimed the vicar. "But what happens if I pull both strings at the same time?"

"I fall off my bloody perch, you w*nker!" screeched the parrot.

A simple-minded man was sitting opposite a priest on the train.

"Excuse me, why do you wear your collar back to front?" asked the man.

"It's because I'm a Father," replied the priest.

"But I'm a father too," said the man, "and I don't wear my collar back to front."

"Aah, but the difference is, I'm a Father to thousands."

"Well in that case," retorted the man, "it's not your collar, it's your trousers you should wear back to front."

A man goes into the confessional and says, "Forgive me, Father, for I have sinned. Yesterday, I cursed badly, using the F-word."
"Why was that?" asked the priest.
"I was playing a round of golf and all was going well until I reached the 10th hole when my tee shot ended up in thick undergrowth."
"Is that when you said the F-word?"
"No, I stayed calm, took my time and hit a clean shot out of the rough, down the fairway, but at the last moment the ball hit a small branch and veered off into the bunker."
"I like a game of golf myself," said the priest, "and that really is annoying. Was that when you used the F-word?"
"No, I tried not to let it get to me. I took my time and hit a beautiful ball up on to the green, only two inches from the hole."

"How frustrating, is that when you used the F-word?"
"No, Father, I still remained calm . . . "
"Don't tell me!" interrupted the priest. "You didn't miss the f*cking putt?!"

The local Catholic priest rang up his opposite number in the Church of England asking him for a favour. "I'm supposed to hear confessions in half-an-hour, but something unexpected has come up and I have to be the other side of the diocese by two o'clock. Will you take over from me here?" asked the priest.

"What? But I've never done it before."

"It's quite straightforward," said the priest. "Sit in with me for half an hour before I go and you'll soon get the hang of it."

So the vicar agreed and was soon hidden away within earshot of the confessional. The first person to enter was a woman.

"Father, I have sinned."

"What have you done, my child?"

"I have been unfaithful."

"How many times have you been unfaithful?"

"Four times, Father, and I am truly sorry."

"Very well. Put £2 in the box and say ten Hail Marys

and you'll be absolved."

Not long after another woman came in.

"Father, I have sinned."

"What have you done, my child?"

"I have slept with a married man."

"How many times?"

"Twice."

"Then put £1 in the box, say five Hail Marys and you'll be absolved."

The priest whispered to the vicar. "You see how it works? Take over from me now, I have to go."

The vicar seated himself in the confessional and immediately a woman sat down on the other side.

"Father, I have sinned," she said.

"What have you done, my child?"

"I have committed adultery."

"How many times?"

"Only once, Father."

"Well, you'd better go back and do it again."

"What! You want me to do it again?"

"Yes, it's two for £1."

"The Canon's here to see you, Bishop."
"Tell him he's fired."

Mother Superior was talking to one of her young nuns. "Sister, if you were out late at night on your own and a man attacked you, what would you do?"

"I would lift up my habit," she replied.

"Goodness me, and then what would you do?"

"I would tell him to drop his pants."

"Oh, Lord save us," gaped the Mother Superior, "and then what?"

"I would run away as fast as I could – and I can run much faster with my habit up, than he can with his trousers down."

'Father, I'm having wicked thoughts.'

A drunk staggers into church and wanders up the aisle moaning to himself. "Jesus Christ, I'm in agony!" Eventually, he makes it into the confessional and all goes quiet. After a few minutes the priest decides he'd better find out if everything is all right so he says, "May I help you, my son?" "I don't know," comes the reply, "it depends on whether you have any loo paper in there."

The story of Adam and Eve has become slightly mistold over the years. As it happens, Eve was created first and God gave her three breasts. But after a while she complained that she was in some pain because they kept bumping against each other, so he agreed to take the middle one away. Time passed and Eve began to get bored so she asked God if he could make her someone to play with.

"Of course," replied God. "I'll call him man . . . now where did I put that useless t*t?"

An old vicar was retiring and selling
his horse so he put an ad in the local
newspaper. It wasn't long before it was
bought by Bob who decided to ride it
home. But when he mounted up, the horse
wouldn't move an inch.

"I trained this horse from a little foal,"
said the vicar. "He only moves when you
say Jesus Christ and stops when you
say Amen."

Bob thanked the vicar and sure enough
when he said "Jesus Christ", the horse set
off. However, on the way home they were
caught in a ferocious thunderstorm and
when there was a particularly loud crack
of thunder the horse bolted. By the time
Bob had recovered his wits, the horse was
galloping madly through the countryside
and it took Bob a moment or two to
remember to say, "Amen!"

Immediately the horse came to a
standstill, teetering right on the edge of a
deep canyon. Bob breathed a sigh of relief.
"Jesus Christ!" he said.

"Excuse me, Vicar," said the man as he walked into church. "I've had my bicycle stolen and I wonder if you would mention in your sermon today how wrong it is to steal. Perhaps the culprit might return it to me?"

"Why, certainly," replied the vicar. "As it happens, I shall be talking about the Ten Commandments, so that will fit in nicely."

"And so I say to you," said the vicar during the service later on, "remember what God taught us. Thou shalt not kill, thou shalt not steal . . . "

Later that week the vicar bumped into the man again as he was wheeling his bicycle down the road.

"Ah, I see my sermon must have worked," remarked the vicar, smiling.

"Oh no, it wasn't that," replied the man. "It was when you got to the bit about not committing adultery that I remembered where I'd left it."

There were some doubts about his wedding. On the great day, his future father-in-law, making polite conversation, said to the vicar, "Why do you rope off the aisles?"

"So the groom can't get away," replied the vicar.

The priest and the Church of England vicar bumped into each other in the public library.

"How funny," said the vicar. "I had a dream last night about a Catholic heaven. It was full of people drinking, singing and dancing."

"Really?" replied the priest. "I had a dream about a Protestant heaven.

It was very peaceful, with beautiful countryside, gorgeous gardens and gently flowing streams."

The vicar smiled contentedly. "And what were the people doing?"

"What people?" replied the priest.

The vicar is preparing for the morning service when he spots a woman, in a very short skirt, sitting in the front pew. He beckons to his deacon and asks, "Isn't that Fanny Blue?"

"Oh, no, I don't think so," replies the deacon. "It's just the way the light is reflected through the stained-glass window."

A devout churchgoer and her 16-year-old daughter attended church every Sunday without fail. One Sunday, the vicar was waiting to greet his parishioners as they left church when he happened to notice a slight bulge in the daughter's stomach.

"Good morning, Mrs Dogood," he said, smiling, "it looks as if your daughter is putting on a little weight."

The woman blushed with discomfort.

"Oh, it's nothing," she replied, "just a little wind."

A few months later, the vicar noticed the girl had got even larger.

"Are you sure everything's all right?" he asked.

"Of course, Vicar," replied the woman, "just a little wind."

The next time the vicar saw the two women, they were walking down the high street, pushing a pram. He stopped to say hello and, bending down to look in the pram, remarked, "So that's the little fart, is it?"

"I don't know what's going on," said worried Bob to his mate.

"Last month we moved parishes and I left our church, which had a message pinned up outside saying, 'Sex is your worst enemy,' only to get to the new church and read, 'Make your worst enemy your best friend.'"

DUTY CALLS

In a distant outpost of the Foreign Legion, one of the more recent recruits confides to his sergeant that lack of female company is driving him round the twist.
"No need to let that worry you, son. Here, let me show you. See that barrel over there, the one with the hole in the side? You'll find it will help relieve the pressure. You're free to use it on Tuesday through to Sunday."
"That's great, thanks. Er . . . but . . . what's wrong with Monday?"
"Well, fair's fair; if you're using it six days a week, then on Monday, it's your turn inside the barrel."

Two retired colonels were bemoaning the younger generation over drinks at their gentlemen's club.
"You'll never believe this," said the first colonel.
"When I told my granddaughter that her grandfather was killed at Waterloo, she wanted to know on which platform!"
"Oh, how ridiculous," replied the second colonel, "as if it mattered what platform he was on!"

The troops were behind enemy lines, holed up in the
basement of an old chateau. Look-outs were placed at
strategic points around the grounds and one of them
gave the alarm signal just before dusk on the sixth day.
"Quick, everyone below," whispered the troop leader.
"Get into the cellar and stay very, very quiet."
They all hid in the basement. All as quiet as mice
except for the constant sound of clink, clink, clink.
"What's that bloody noise?" exclaimed the leader.
"Hobbs, see to it pronto."
A few minutes passed, the noise stopped and
Hobbs returned.
"What was it?" they asked.
"Mitchell, sir, in the old toilet, w*nking," replied Hobbs.
"Good man, Hobbs. You stopped him then?"
"No, sir. I removed the brass buttons on his cuffs."

**Police have announced they would like
to interview a man wearing high heels
and black lace knickers.
But the chief constable has stated that
they must wear their uniforms instead.**

A visiting general was inspecting the troops out on manoeuvres in the middle of nowhere. As he passed a small group of soldiers, carefully disguised as trees, one of them made a sudden movement.

"Now, soldier," said the general sternly, "if you move like that, you'll blow the cover of everyone."

"Sorry, sir," stammered the distressed soldier. "Yesterday, I stayed stock still when two crows started to build a nest in my top branches.

Today, I didn't move a muscle when a dog peed up against my trunk. But sir, when I heard two squirrels say, 'Let's get the two nuts and take them back to our nest,' I just had to do something."

The troops were out on manoeuvres in the Himalayas, when one of the animals carrying their supplies collapsed and died.

"You two men there," shouted the corporal, "bury this animal immediately."

As the men dug the hole, one remarked to the other, "Poor old donkey."

"That's not a donkey, that's a mule," said his mate.

Neither could agree so they asked the opinion of

a third soldier.
"Trust me, lads," he said, "that's an ass."
Some time later, just as they were finishing off
the hole, a passing colonel stopped to speak.
"Is that a foxhole you're digging, men?"
he asked.
"No, sir," replied the men saluting, "we're digging
an asshole."

The court martial pronounced the private guilty as charged and ordered him to be taken from the court to a place where he would face the firing squad. As the troops escorted the prisoner on the two-mile trek to the execution area, the heavens opened and it rained furiously.
"Bloody awful weather," moaned the prisoner. "All this bloody way, soaking wet, freezing cold, just to be shot."
"Shut up, will you," replied one of the soldiers. "At least you don't have to walk all the way back in it."

A man walked into a police station to report
that his wife had gone missing.

"She went out about four hours ago and she hasn't been back to cook my dinner so I know there must be something wrong."

"OK, sir, let's not panic. I'll just take down some details. Can you describe your wife, what she was wearing when she left the house?"

"No, I can't think how to describe her, but I did see her walking down the road with our next-door neighbour, and she's not back either."

"I don't suppose you can give us a description of her?"

"Oh, yes, she's about 5ft 6in, black shoulder-length curly hair, 36-24-36, wearing a red mini skirt and a red-and-white jacket."

One day while on traffic control, a policeman flags down a car for speeding. As he walks up to the car he sees it is being driven by a beautiful brunette. "Excuse me, Miss, did you not see the signs? This is a 30mph zone and you were going at least 50mph. I'll need to see your licence and insurance, please."

"Oh, dear," replies the dizzy girl. "Do you mean these, officer?"

She hands him some documents from the glove compartment.

"That's right, Miss, won't be a moment." With that he walks over to his car to radio in the details.

"I think I know this woman," comes the reply. "Is she a dizzy brunette?"

"Yes, why?"

"Just go back over and take your trousers down."

"What the f*ck are you talking about?" says the policeman in amazement.

"Don't worry, just do as I say, it'll be fine."

So the policeman turns round and returns to the woman's car, hands back her documents and then suddenly drops his trousers.

"Oh no," sighs the girl, "not another breathalyzer."

*'We're looking for a thief who smells nice.
She got him with her perfume not her mace.'*

A music hall entertainer is stopped by the police for having a faulty brake light. On the back seat of the car, the policeman spots a whole set of knives. He asks the man why he has them – doesn't he know it's against the law to carry knives?
The man explains that the knives are used in his act – he juggles them.
The policeman insists the man gets out to show him, so he gets out and stands at the roadside performing his act. Just then, another car drives by and the driver turns to his wife saying, "Thank God I gave up the drinking, those tests get tougher every day!"

The traffic police spotted a man staggering towards his car and opening the driver's door. They stopped and confronted him.
"Excuse me, sir, but I hope you are not intending to drive the car?"
"Of course I am, officer," he slurred. "I'm in no state to walk."

"What's wrong, Miss?" asked the kindly policeman when he saw the girl crying. "A thief has just stolen £20 I had hidden in my knickers," she sobbed. "Did you try to stop him?" "I didn't know he was only after my money."

The ticket inspector was checking tickets on the 4.30 to Bath when she was stopped by a man who opened his raincoat and flashed his tackle.

"Oh, no, that's no good," she replied with vigour. "I want to see your ticket, not just the stub."

The traffic police flagged down a car. "Excuse me, sir, you've just hit four parked cars and driven straight over the middle of the roundabout. It's obvious you are very drunk." "Officer, thank you so much for telling me. I thought the steering had gone on the car."

UP BEFORE THE BEAK

A man is up before the courts for walking down the
high street completely naked.
"Is it true that you didn't have a stitch on?" asks
the judge.
"That's right, Your Honour."
"Well, have you no shame? Are you married?"
"Yes, Your Honour."
"And how many children do you have?"
"Sixteen, Your Honour."
"Release this man, he was only in his work clothes."

*"Maurice Highton, you are up before this
court for shooting your wife. Do you
have anything to say?"*

*"Yes, Your Honour," he replied without
hesitation. "She told me that I was a
really dreadful lover."*

"And you killed her for saying that?"

*"No," he answered, angrily. "I killed her
for knowing the difference."*

A policeman was on the beat late one night when he spotted a car parked up a side alley. He shone his torch through the back window and saw a young couple playing Scrabble.

"What's going on here?" he demanded.

"We're just playing Scrabble," replied the boy.

"That's an odd thing to do at this time of night," he said, looking suspiciously at the girl.

"And how old are you?" he asked.

She looked up at the church clock and replied happily, "In ten minutes' time I'll be 16."

A crafty barrister was defending a beautiful, shapely blonde accused of fraud and in his final address he turned to the all-male jury and said, "Gentlemen, are we going to see this poor, very friendly woman spend the next few years in jail or should she return to her private and secluded flat at 48 Green Walk, telephone number 491 7360?"

"Before I pass sentence have you anything to say?"
demanded the judge.
"F*ck all," came the insolent reply.
The judge turned to one of the court officials and said,
"I didn't hear that; what did he say?"
"He said, 'F*ck all', Your Honour," whispered
the official.
"Oh, that's odd. I'm sure I saw his lips move."

Judge to husband: "I'm awarding your wife £300 a month."
"Well, that's very generous, Your Honour. I'll try to chip in a couple of pounds myself."

"Good morning, I'm a criminal lawyer," said the man to
his new client.
"Oh well, at least you're not ashamed about describing
yourself," came the reply.

A man was up before the court on a charge of vagrancy. He had lost his job, house and family and fallen on hard times.

The judge found him guilty as charged, and looked down at him in the dock.

"Young man, it is drink and drink alone that has brought you before this court today."

On hearing this, the young man cheered up considerably.

"Oh, thank you, Your Honour, everyone else says it's my fault."

"Mr Makepiece, you are up before this court for possessing a counterfeit press. Although no money can be found, I pronounce you guilty of intent to produce counterfeit money. Do you have anything to say?" asked the judge.

"Just one thing, Your Honour. You'd better find me guilty of adultery as well because I have the equipment for that too."

The judge said to the drunk, "Please stand, Mr Havermore. Before passing sentence, I need to know if you are sober enough to understand you have been brought here for drinking."
"Oh, that's very kind, Your Honour, but I'm trying to give it up, you see."

"I want a divorce," said the woman to her lawyer.
"And can you tell me why?" he asked.
"Because each night in bed my husband lets out this bloodcurdling scream every time he reaches a climax."
The lawyer blushed profusely and said, "But . . . er . . . surely that's quite normal, isn't it?"
"Not when it wakes me up every night," she retorted.

"You didn't stop at the last junction," said the policeman to the motorist. "I'll have to breathalyze you." He held up the bag.
"What's that?" asked the driver.
"This tells you if you've had too much to drink," the copper replied.

"Well, I never!" he exclaimed. "I'm married to one of those."

"Luigi, Luigi," shouted the children as they lined up for the ice-cream van. But Luigi was nowhere to be seen. The motor was running, the music was playing but no one was serving.

"Stand back, kids," said a policeman. He peered inside the van and saw Luigi lying on the floor covered in chocolate sauce, mixed nuts and fresh cream.

"Sarge," he said, speaking into his radio. "This is PC Mann, I need some back-up at the ice-cream van on Prospect Street. It's Luigi – he's topped himself."

Our town was so lawless, if you went to buy a pair of tights, they'd ask you for your head size.

A man was relieving himself in some bushes just as a policeman walked by.

"What the hell are you doing?" the copper demanded angrily. "There's a public toilet just down there."

"It may be big," retorted the man, "but it's not a bloody hose pipe!"

Did you hear about the humiliated flasher? His case was heard in the Small Claims Court.

"And where do you think you're going at this time of night?" the police officer asked the staggering drunk.
"To a lecture," the man replied.
"Come off it. It's one o'clock in the morning. Who'd be giving a lecture at this late hour?"
"My wife."

A man was in court for killing his wife. The jury was made up mainly of women so he felt his chances of getting off were very slim. But he was quite handsome, so in desperation he decided to try to seduce one of the women on the jury and persuade her to reduce his verdict to manslaughter. He succeeded and when the trial came to an end, the jury

left to consider their verdict. A few hours later they returned and found him guilty of manslaughter. Relieved, the man thanked the woman for all she'd done.
"Well, it wasn't easy," she replied. "The others wanted to acquit you."

The judge said to the farmer: "Mr Brown, you are here to claim damages against this truck driver for the awful injuries you sustained at the time of the accident. And yet, Mr Brown, you were heard to say to the policeman that you'd never felt better. Kindly explain."

"It's like this, Your Honour," replied the farmer. "At the time of the accident the policeman went over to my dog and saw it was badly injured, so he shot it. Then he went over to my two cows and saw they had broken legs, so he shot them as well. When he came to me, I thought it a good idea to tell him I'd never felt better."

A simple man accused of stalking a beautiful young girl was told he would have to line up in an identity parade.
When they took the girl along the line, he shouted loudly, "That's her!"

A BIT ON THE SIDE

A tall, handsome man pops into the vet's and asks the receptionist how long he will have to wait.

"Oh, about 30 minutes, Mr Wellbeing has two cats and a gerbil to see."

"Thank you," replies the man and walks out. Over the next few weeks, the man appears several times, asks the same question and then leaves. By this time, the receptionist is so intrigued, she tells the vet and he suggests that the next time the man comes in she should follow him when he leaves.

So the receptionist does as she's asked and, on returning, says to the vet, "Well, it's very strange. All he seems to do is go straight round to your house."

"How do you like my new suit?" said Steve to his friend.

"Wow! that must have cost a lot of money."

"I don't know, it was a present from my wife. When I arrived home early yesterday afternoon, it was hanging over the bottom of the bed."

"Mabel, that milkman will have to go," said the enraged husband. "He's so cheeky, he reckons he's slept with every woman on this street, except one."
"Oh, I know who that'll be," replied his wife, "that stuck-up cow at number 32."

☞ ★ ☜

"I'm sorry to hear your Bert's in hospital, I heard it was his knee."
"That's right, I found a blonde sitting on it."

'Phil, I think you might have got the wrong idea about this fantasy football.'

The phone rings and the husband answers it.
"No, mate, you want the Met office."
"Who was that, darling?" asks the wife.
"I don't know, I think he wanted the weather forecast, because he asked me if the coast was clear."

"You never make a noise or cry out when you have an orgasm,"
he complained.
"How would you know? You're never there," she retorted.

Following a night of fantastic sex with a woman he picked up in the pub, the man is afraid to go home and face his wife, knowing that he's terrible at lying.
"I have a great idea," says the woman. "Stick these darts in your back pocket and tell her the truth. Trust me, it will be all right."
So, with trepidation, the man returns home to find his wife in the kitchen waiting for him.
"OK," she hisses, "where the hell have you been this time?"
"I've been making wonderful love to a beautiful

woman, all night long," he replies.
"You bloody liar, pull the other one! You've been with
your mates playing darts, I can see them in your
back pocket."

*The angry woman marched round to
her next-door neighbour's house
and confronted her with a set of
photographs.*
*"Look at these, you common tart, this
is proof that you've been seeing my
husband. There's one of the two of you
in bed, this is a picture of you and him
in the back seat of the car and this
one shows you sitting on his knee. What
do you have to say for yourself?"*
*For a few moments, the next-
door neighbour looked through the
photographs and then said, "Mmm, not
bad, I'll have two copies of the first
picture and one each of the other two."*

Old Jake only had moments to live. At his bedside were his family – his wife and four sons, three of whom had blond hair, the other ginger.

"Mavis, I've always wondered why one of our sons had red hair. Tell me truthfully, is he really my son?"

Mavis put her hand on her heart and swore fervently that, yes, he was his son.

"Oh, thank goodness," croaked the old man and he died with a smile on his face.

As the family left the room, the wife sighed deeply, "Thank heaven he didn't ask about the other three."

An artist and his sexy model were canoodling in the conservatory when they heard her husband's car drive up. "Quick," whispered the artist. "Take your clothes off so it looks like we're working."

The couple had been married a year when the husband was called away on business to the other side of the country. It would mean he would be away for a month so the wife's friend moved in to keep her company. As it happened, the job finished earlier than expected so he jumped on a plane and, on landing, rang his wife from the airport. Her friend answered the phone to say that Tracy was in the bath.

"OK, can you tell her I'll be there about midnight so if she can wear something sexy we'll make it a night to remember."

"OK," said the friend, "and who shall I say called?"

'This will get the neighbours talking.'

The old farmer married a young girl of 18 and after a few months of idyllic married life, he went to see his doctor.

"The problem is I'm having to work many hours on the farm, but I have to keep breaking off when I get the urge, to run back to the house, jump into bed and do the business. Then it's back to work, and it's knackering me."

The doctor suggested that his wife should come to see him out in the fields.

"Every time you get the urge," said the doctor, "fire a shot from your gun to let your wife know you're waiting for her."

A few months passed and then the doctor met the old farmer in the high street.

"How's the shotgun plan working?" he asked.

"Oh, it was very good at first, but then the duck-shooting season started and I haven't seen her since," he replied sadly.

The little boy's mum had shaved off all her pubic hair, ready to wear her skimpy bikini when they went on holiday.

"Where's all your hair gone?" asked her son.

"I've lost my sponge," she replied dismissively, and told him to go out to play. Sometime later he returned with a big smile on his face.

"Mummy, Mummy, am I a good boy for finding your sponge?"

Puzzled, Mum asked him where it was and he answered her proudly, "The lady across the road is washing Daddy's face with it."

A man comes home early to find his wife in bed with another man.

"Who the bloody hell's this?" he shouts angrily.

"Good question," she replies. "Say, lover, what's your name?"

"Do you talk to your wife when you're making love?"
"Only if she rings up."

The simple man was beside himself with anger when he discovered his wife in bed with another man.

"How could you?" he yelled and, taking a gun out of the bottom drawer of the bedside table, he placed it to his head and cocked the trigger.

"Don't, Jim, please don't," sobbed the woman, "put the gun down."

"Say your prayers, you're next," snapped the man.

'If you want my body and you think I'm sexy...'

A woman was in bed with her lover when she heard her husband open the front door.

"Quick!" she whispered urgently. "It's my husband, hide in the wardrobe."

The man climbed in. "Ooh, it's dark in here," said a little voice.

"Who's that?" gasped the man.

"That's my mum you were with and I'm going to call my dad."

"Now, now, son, not so hasty, I'm sure we can work this out."

"OK," said the small boy. "But it's going to cost you."

"How about £5?"

"I'm going to call Dad."

"Well £10 then."

"I'm going to call Dad."

"OK, let's say £20."

"No, £30."

"Well, that's all I've got, here you are." The man handed over the money and made his escape when the coast was clear.

A few days later, Mum took the little boy to church and as she knelt to pray he wandered off and crept into the confessional.

"Ooh, it's dark in here," he said.

"Don't start that again!" replied the agitated priest.

A man came home early from work to find his wife in bed with another man. The man's head was laying between the wife's voluptuous breasts.

"What the f*ck are you doing?" shouted the husband.

"Listening to some good music," replied the man calmly.

"Get off, let me hear," demanded the husband, but when he put his head between his wife's breasts he couldn't hear anything.

"Of course not," replied the other man arrogantly. "You're not plugged in."

After partying most of the night, a young couple woke up the next day with awful hangovers.

"I'm sorry, love," said the husband, "but was it you I made love to last night in the spare bedroom?"

"I don't know," she replied. "What position did we use?"

A man turns to his friend and asks him why he's looking so puzzled. He replies, "I've received this letter today and it's from a man who says he'll beat me senseless if I don't stay away from his wife."
"So what's puzzling you?"
"Well, he hasn't signed it."

When a man arrives home from work one evening he's greeted by his wife, who's got a bottle of hair conditioner in her hand.
"What's that for?" he asks. "My hair's OK."
"Yours maybe, but this is for your girlfriend whose hair keeps coming out all over your shoulders!"

"I want to divorce my husband," said the shapely brunette to her solicitor.
"On what grounds?"
"Infidelity, he's not the father of my child."

A man comes home early from work to find his wife in bed. He's immediately suspicious and opens the wardrobe to find her lover hiding amongst the clothes, stark naked.

"What are you doing in there?" demands the angry husband.

"I'm the local pest controller," stumbles the man, "and we've heard there's an infestation of moths about . . . "

"So how come you're bollock naked?" shouts the husband.

"Well, bugger me!" replies the man in amazement as he looks down at his body. "This infestation's worse than I thought!"

A man came home early from work to find his wife in bed with a strange man. "Let me explain," she said. "He came to the door looking for something to eat, so I gave him the breakfast you didn't want this morning. Then he asked if there were any clothes I didn't want, so I gave him your old blue suit that was going to the jumble sale. At that point he asked if there was anything else you didn't use."

"When I came home from work last night, I found my wife in bed with another man. How can I stop this happening again?"

"Work more overtime."

"And do you know," said the simple man, "she loves me so much. Last week I was off sick. Every morning she was so glad to have me home she'd run out into the street when the milkman or postman arrived, shrieking, 'My husband's here, my husband's at home!' "

Jack and Bill are in the urinals. On seeing Bill's prick, Jack exclaims, "How did you get such a huge prick?"

"Oh that's easy," replies Bill proudly. "Every night before I get into bed I knock it five times on the bottom of the bed."

That night Jack decides to do the same and before getting into bed knocks his prick on the bottom of the bed five times.

Awakened by the noise, his wife whispers, "Is that you, Bill?"

A woman goes to her doctor's for a check-up.
After examining her, he gives her the unwelcome news that she is pregnant. She is shattered by this, and immediately rings her husband.
"I'm pregnant, you b*stard, why didn't you wear a condom?" she yells.
"Now, hold on a minute," he replies.
"I always wear a condom. Anyway, who is this?"

Jack Carter, chairman of an international company, arrives at work one winter's morning only to find that someone has peed in the snow outside his office window. Not just peed, in fact, but formed the words: "Jack Carter – big a**ehole."
Outraged, he immediately calls in his private secretary and demands that the culprits be discovered.
Later, the secretary returns and rather nervously gives him the news. "Sir, the urine belongs to the deputy chairman, but . . . er . . . "
"But what, man, come on, but what?"
"Well, sir, the handwriting belongs to your wife."

Gerald had had a dreadful argument with his wife, and he'd said some unforgivable things – not least that she was no bloody good in bed. He decided to ring her up to apologize.

It took ages for her to answer the phone, but finally she did.

"Oh, June, it's me," he said. "Where were you?"

"I was in bed," she replied.

"In bed!" he exclaimed, "In the middle of the day? Why?"

She thought for a moment and replied, "I was just getting a second opinion."

What is a vindictive pregnancy?
Someone who's had it in for you while you've been away.

"What the hell's going on here?" yelled the angry husband, on going out into the garden to smell the roses

and finding his wife and the gardener canoodling in the summer house. "You see," said his wife scornfully, "I told you he was stupid."

A couple are having it away on the sofa when the phone rings. After answering it, she replaces the receiver and turns to her lover, saying, "It was only my husband."

'I quite like sex, but you're not too keen, are you, dear?'

"Oh, no," replies the man, "I'd better get out of here."
"Don't worry, he won't be home for hours, he's playing
pool with you and two other mates."

☞ ★ ☜

*"Mum, Dad, I have something to tell
you. I'm marrying Julie from the shop."
"That's wonderful news," says Mum.
"Er . . . yes . . . " says Dad.
Later, when they are on their own, Dad
confesses to his son that he had an
extra-marital affair and that Julie is his
half-sister. The boy is devastated. He
breaks off the engagement. Two years
later, he comes home again.
"Mum, Dad, I've asked Tracy to marry
me and she's accepted."
Again, Dad doesn't say much until later.
"I'm sorry, son, I did have another fling
and Tracy is also your half-sister."
The boy gets angry and decides to tell
his mother the awful truth.
"Don't worry about your father," she
says. "What he doesn't know is that
he's not really your dad."*

IN THE SACK

She took him up to her bedroom and while he waited for her to slip into something more comfortable he noticed her room was piled high with all sorts of cuddly toys. But that was soon forgotten once they started to make love. After it was over he turned to her and said smugly, "How was it for you?" "Not bad, I suppose," she replied, "you can pick anything from the bottom shelf."

A young man asks for shelter for the night when his car breaks down in the middle of nowhere. An old couple invite him in, apologize for only having two bedrooms – one for them and the other for their daughter, Ida – but offer him the sofa for the night. Around 4 o'clock, it turns cold and the woman comes down to see if he's all right.

"Would you like our eiderdown?" she asks.

"Oh, no, no thank you!" he exclaims. "She's been down twice already."

A woman went to her vicar to seek advice on her forthcoming wedding. This was to be her third husband and she was not sure how to tell him that she was still a virgin.

"But how can that be?" exclaimed the vicar. "You've already had two husbands."

"That's true, but my first husband was a psychiatrist and all he did was talk about it, my second husband was a gynaecologist and all he did was look at it. But this time I'm sure it will be different. This time I'm marrying a lawyer so I'm sure to get screwed."

"How dare you ask me if I've been to bed with anyone else – that's my business!" she said angrily.

"I'm sorry, I didn't know you were a professional," replied the young man.

"It's no good, it's over," said Julie.
"You are so bad in bed."
"Oh, come on!" said the man affronted.
"How can you tell after 15 seconds?"

A man and a woman start to have sex in the middle of a dark forest. After 15 minutes, the man gets up, shaking his head, and says, "Damn, I wish I had a torch."
The woman says, "So do I. You've been eating grass for the past ten minutes."

'Tch... his idea of foreplay is to take his socks off.'

Knowing her husband wouldn't be home till late, the woman brought her lover back to the house for some frolics.
"Hold on, I can't," her lover said suddenly, "I've forgotten to bring the condoms."
"Oh that's alright, my husband's got some."
But after searching for them for five minutes, she returned angrily to the bedroom.
"The bugger's taken them with him, I knew he didn't trust me."

Did you hear about the man who had "I love you" tattooed on his d*ck? That night in bed, he turned to his wife and said, "What do you think of this, Beryl?" "There you go again!" she exclaimed, "always trying to put words in my mouth."

JUST MARRIED

It was decided that the newlyweds would spend their honeymoon night with her parents. But the walls were very thin and Mum and Dad were disturbed by all the humping noises.
Eventually the father had a good idea. "I know," he said, "every time they do it, so will we."
After an hour, the honeymooners went quiet and everyone fell asleep.
But two hours later they started again and after 45 minutes, quiet was restored and the parents fell into an exhausted sleep. However, around dawn, activity began again and the father was forced to shout out, "Stop it, you're killing your mother!"

Chris and Lucy had been courting for three years but they'd never been intimate because he had a wooden leg and could never tell her about it. They decided to

get married and on the momentous day, Chris realized
he was going to have to tell Lucy the truth, but still
he chickened out. That night, when they got into the
bedroom, Chris turned to Lucy and said, "Lucy, darling,
I've got a big secret and I guess it's time I told you
what it was."

With that, he switched off the light, stripped off,
and detached his wooden leg. "Here," he whispered,
handing her the leg.

"Oooh," she chuckled. "You old devil, now this is what I
<u>call</u> a surprise."

*'You want to marry me, Norman? Oh my
gosh, are you sure?!!'*

A young newlywed couple were staying with his folks, but when they went to bed that night they were unable to allow their passions to erupt for fear of making too much noise.
"Let's go to a hotel," he suggested.
So they packed the suitcase, but had trouble closing the lid.
Next door, the father heard her say, "Let me sit on it," and a moment later he heard his son say, "Let's both sit on it."
Amazed, the father jumped out of bed and rushed to the door, saying, "I've just got to see this!"

A couple on their honeymoon ask for a suite in the local hotel.
The clerk asks them if they want the bridal.
"No, that's alright," replies the groom. "I'll hold on to her ears until she gets the hang of it.

It was their honeymoon night. The Reverend Johns and his new wife retired to the honeymoon suite and he disappeared into the bathroom to get ready. When he came out, his wife was already in bed.

"Oh, Mabel, I thought you'd be on your knees," he said.

"Oh, we can do it that way later. For the moment, I just want to see your face," she replied.

"Now you've just got married, let me tell you about sex," said the man's father.

"You go through three different stages. First of all, when you're newlyweds, you have sex anytime, anywhere – the kitchen, the bedroom, the garage, whenever the urge takes you. But then, when you've been married for a while, you usually keep sex to the bedroom – that's stage two. Stage three comes after many years of marriage. It's when you pass each other in the hall and say, 'F*ck you!'"

It was seven days into their honeymoon and the young bride staggered downstairs to breakfast looking absolutely knackered.

"My goodness," said the waitress. "You don't look so good, but aren't you the bride with the older husband?"

"Yes, I am, and he's 75, but I've discovered he's pulled a dreadful trick on me. When he told me he had saved up for 50 years, I thought he was talking about money."

To encourage her naive young husband to be more exciting in bed, the young wife bought a pair of crotchless knickers. At the time he was due home from work, she lay on the bed with her legs apart and said to him as he came through the door,

"Hello, darling, fancy a bit of this?"

"Argh! No, thanks!" he said, horrified. "Just look what it's done to your panties."

Gerald decided to marry for a second time. He'd been a successful businessman and lived a very happy life, but his wife of 35 years had died and he was lonely. For some time, he'd been dating a girl 20 years his junior and he felt the time was right to pop the question.

"Well . . . " she hesitated. "There are a few things I'd insist upon."

"Just name them, my dear," he replied.

"First of all, I'd want my own monthly account."

"It's yours," he replied.

"And I'd like my own car."

"Certainly," he said.

She paused for a moment and then said "And what about sex?"

"Oh, infrequently," he replied, blushing.

She mused on this for a moment or two and then continued, "Is that one word or two?"

IT'S OVER!

The couple had been married for seven years and were going through a bad patch. They agreed to see a marriage counsellor and, a few minutes into the interview, the counsellor took the wife in his arms and kissed her passionately.

"Now, that's what your wife needs," he explained to the astonished husband. "More passion. Tuesday, Thursday and Friday every week."

The husband thought for a moment and replied grudgingly, "Well, OK then. But I can't bring her in on Fridays – it's darts night."

A woman comes home to find her husband crying his eyes out.

"My goodness, what's wrong?" she asks.

He looks up at her and says, "Do you remember 15 years ago when I got you pregnant? Your father was so flamin' angry he said I had to marry you or go to jail?"

"Yes, I remember," she replies, "but why are you thinking of that now?"

"Well, today is the day I would have been released!"

A married couple are driving down the motorway doing 55 mph. The wife is behind the wheel. Her husband looks over at her and says, "I know we've been married for 15 years, but I want a divorce."

The wife says nothing but speeds up to 60 mph.

He then says, "I don't want you to try to talk me out of it, because I've been having an affair with your best friend, and she's a better lover than you."

Again the wife stays silent, her speed increasing.

"I want the house," he says.

Again the wife speeds up, and is now doing 70mph.

"I want the kids, too," he says.

The wife just keeps driving faster and faster – now she's up to 80mph.

"I want the car, the bank account and all the credit cards," he continues.

As he says, "Is there anything you want?", his wife veers towards the concrete base of a huge flyover.

"No, I've got everything I need," says the wife.

"What's that?" he asks.

Just before they hit the wall at 90mph, the wife replies, "I've got the airbag!"

Randy Ron, his workmates called him. He just couldn't get enough.

One afternoon he came home early from work, went straight up to the bedroom to change and found his wife in bed with the covers pulled right over her head.

Not one to miss a chance, he stripped off, crept under the covers and hastily made love to her. Later he got up and went downstairs, only to discover his wife in the garden.

"How can you be down here?" he demanded. "I just left you in bed."

"No, that's my mother, she wasn't feeling so well so I told her to lie down."

The man turned pale and sat down shaking. "Bloody hell, I've just made love to your mother!"

"Oh no," she gasped, running upstairs. "Mum, Mum, why didn't you say something?"

Her mother replied with affront, "I haven't spoken to that randy bugger for three years and I'm not about to start now."

Did you hear about the girl who advertised for a husband in the personal column of the local paper? She had over 200 replies saying, "You can have mine."

☛ ★ ☚

"Oh, sure," said the frustrated wife. "My husband's a winner all right! When it comes to lovemaking, he always finishes first."

'Right... do you find me a/. very sexy b/. sexy c/. not sexy at all?'

SWEET NOTHINGS

"I love you very much," said the ardent young lover. "I may not have much money, like my mate Martin, I may not have a sports car or a cottage in the country like him. But I love you with all my heart and everything I have is yours."

"Very nice," she replied, preoccupied, "but tell me a little more about Martin."

The young girl stormed back into the flat looking very angry.
"What's up with you?" asked her friend.
"It's my new boyfriend, Colin. I had to slap his face four times tonight."
"Really?" she exclaimed. "Trying it on all the time, is he?"
"No," she retorted. "The bugger keeps falling asleep."

She was so naive the man tricked her into marrying him by telling her she was pregnant.

"*Doctor, doctor, I think there's something terribly wrong,*" *said the agitated man. He went on to describe his symptoms.*

"*The first time I made love, I felt warm and restful and comfortable all over. But the second time I couldn't stop shivering, I was so cold and covered in goose pimples.*"

"*Mmm,*" *replied the doctor,* "*that sounds very unusual, I'd better give you a thorough examination.*"

But nothing seemed amiss so the doctor sent for the man's wife and told her about the odd complaint.

"*He felt warm and comfortable the first time, but cold and shivery the second.*"

The wife snorted with contempt. "*I'm not surprised,*" *she said.* "*The first time was in summer and the second time was in mid-December!*"

A young man had been going out with his girlfriend
for two months and decided he would like to buy her
a present, but something that was not too personal in
case she thought he was getting too serious.
Unsure of what to buy, he asked his sister to go with
him to the shops and after looking around, he decided
to buy some gloves. As the young man made the
purchase, his sister also did some shopping and bought
a pair of knickers. Unfortunately, in wrapping up the
two purchases, the attendant got them muddled up so
the young man got the knickers. He never thought to
check, but simply wrote a letter to go with the gift and
posted the parcel that evening. His letter read:
"My darling Debs,
Hope you like this little gift. I bought them because
I noticed you didn't wear any when we go out in the
evenings. My sister would have chosen the long ones,
but I think the shorter ones are easier to get off.
I hope the colour's to your liking. The shop assistant
had a pair the same colour and she showed me the
ones she'd been wearing for the past two months and
they were hardly soiled. She was very helpful.
She tried yours on for me so that I could see what they
looked like. I wish I could be there when you first put
them on, but as I'm not meeting you until Saturday I
suppose others will see them before I do.
Until then, all my love, Dave.

P.S. The shop assistant also gave me a little tip. When
you take them off, blow in them before putting them
away as they will be a little damp from wearing,
of course." "

As a thank you to his father's estate
workers, the eldest son would dress up
as Father Christmas each year and visit
every house.
This year, he arrived at the third house
with his sackful of toys and tiptoed into
the bedroom, only to be confronted by
a beautiful young
woman who sat up in bed when she
heard his footsteps.
"Oh, I'm so sorry," said Father
Christmas, looking round the door.
"I thought this was Bobby's room."
"No, he's next door," she whispered.
"But don't go, stay awhile," and with
that she dropped the sheet to reveal a
see-through nightie.
"No, no," said Father Christmas

blushing, *"I've got a busy night ahead of me."*

"Oh, come on," she urged, slowly disrobing. *"A few more minutes won't make that much difference."*

"I'm sorry, I can't," he replied, now feeling very hot under the collar.

"Oh, please," she said, jumping, naked, out of bed.

"Oh, bugger it!" he exclaimed, putting down the sack of toys.

"I wouldn't get back up the chimney like this anyway."

'We met through our involvement in care in the community.'

The snow was thick on the ground when May and her boyfriend, Tom, got stranded miles from anywhere with engine trouble.

"Don't worry," said Tom. "I know about cars, I'm sure I can fix it."

After tinkering around with the engine for a few minutes he got back into the car and put his hands between her legs saying,

"My hands are so cold I can't work on the engine properly, so I'm just warming them up."

A few minutes later he got back out and continued to mend the car, but every so often got back in to warm up his hands between her legs.

When some time had passed and he got into the car again, she turned to him and said, "It's a pity your ears never get cold!"

A courting couple in Lovers Lane have been kissing feverishly for quite some time when the man, unable to contain himself any longer, sticks his d*ck in the girl's hand. She leaps out of the car, shouting loudly, "I've only two words to say to you – p*ss off!"

The man screams back, "I've only got two words to say to you – let go!"

Out on their first date, a young man drove his girlfriend out into the country in his old sports car. However, after labouring slowly up a steep hill, the car suddenly made some strange noises and came to a halt.

"Shall we get out and push it up?" he said.

"OK, but will it be all right to leave the car here?"

A rather shy young man went along to the village dance and met up with a pretty girl. His chat-up lines were sadly lacking, so in blind panic he said the only thing he could think of.

"You're Scottish, aren't you?"

"Aye, I am, how did ye know that?"

"It's the way you roll your Rs."

"Oh, no," she said. "It's these high-heeled shoes that do that."

"Oh, my darling," whispered the passionate young man. "Am I the first man you've ever made love to?"

"Yes, yes," she replied, looking bored. "Why do men always ask the same silly question?"

A young hitchhiker got a lift with a lorry driver, but halfway through the night they found themselves stranded on top of the moors. The driver told her they'd have to wait till morning before getting help, so she could have his bed in the cabin and he would sleep on the seat. After a while, the girl whispered, "It's a shame you have to give up your bed, why don't you come in with me, there's plenty of room."

So the man got in beside her.

"It might be nice if we slept 'married'," she giggled.

"Whatever you like," he said, and he turned his back to her and went to sleep.

When she asked him if he fancied something from the **Kama Sutra**, he replied, "Thanks, but not for me. Indian food has me on the toilet all night."

"I'm getting a divorce," said Jack to his mate Bill. "The wife hasn't spoken to me for six months."
Bill thought for a moment and replied, "Just make sure you know what you're doing, Jack. Wives like that are hard to find."

A married couple are in bed one night when he turns to her and says, "Darling, I've got a new position for us to try. We must lie back to back."
"But I don't understand," she says, "how can that be?"
"It's OK. We've got another couple joining us."

She was only an architect's daughter, but she let the borough surveyor.

"You know, John, as soon as I get home I'm going to tear the wife's bra off. The elastic's killing me."

Is it true that a man who goes to sleep with a sex problem on his mind will wake up in the morning with the answer in his hand?

What do you get if you cross a rooster with
a disobedient dog?
A cock that doesn't come.

**Why do firemen have bigger balls than
policemen?
They sell more tickets.**

What is a woman's belly button for?
It's somewhere to put your chewing gum on the
way down.

*Adam came first.
But then men always do.*

AT THE SURGERY

The dog breeder was advised that if she wanted
a 'champion', some of the dog's hair needed to be
removed from its underside. She went along to the
chemist and asked for some hair remover.
"This is the most efficient product," said the chemist,
showing her a small tube of cream, "but it's advisable
to keep your arms up in the air for at least two minutes
before taking it off."
"Oh, no, you misunderstand me," said the woman,
blushing. "It's for my chihuahua."
"Oh, I see," he replied, "that's no problem, just don't
ride a bike for a couple of hours afterwards."

*"Doctor, doctor, I'm so worried," said the anxious
man. "Both my wife and I have black hair, but
our son's been born with red hair. Do you think
something funny has been going on?"
"Not necessarily," replied the doctor. "How many
times do you have sex?"
"About five times a year."
"Well, there's your answer then, you're just
a little rusty."*

"Mrs Smith, I have some very bad news for you, concerning your husband. We've had the tests back and it shows that he only has hours to live. I'm afraid he'll probably be dead by tomorrow morning."

The poor woman goes home in a terrible state of shock, but she is determined to make his last few hours the best he's ever had. That night, she suggests they go upstairs early and, wearing her sexiest nightie, she lures him into bed and makes love to him like he's never experienced before. After two hours, they lie back exhausted and fall asleep. But half an hour later, the husband wakes up, nudges his wife and tells her it was so wonderful, can they do it again? This happens all night long until the poor wife hardly has the strength to move. As dawn breaks, he whispers yet again, "Just once more, darling, please."

"It's all right for you," she snaps back at him. "You don't have to get up in the morning."

The doctor pointed to a jar on the shelf in his surgery and said, "I want you to fill that."
"What?" gasped the patient.
"From here?"

A very small woman went to the doctor's complaining that her fanny was painful. After a complete examination, the puzzled doctor could find nothing wrong.

"Do you have this pain all the time?" he asked.

"No, only when it's wet outside."

"OK, well, next time it rains come to see me," he suggested.

The following week it rained heavily and the woman appeared once more at the surgery. Again the doctor examined her and immediately discovered the problem.

"Just lie there a moment," he said, "while I find some scissors."

A moment later she sighed with relief. "Oh, doctor, the pain's gone. It's wonderful, what did you do?"

"Oh, quite simple really. I just trimmed an inch off the top of your wellingtons."

"Just go over to the window and stick your tongue out," said the doctor to his patient.

"Why?"

"Because I don't like the man across the road."

A young couple, finding themselves with nowhere to go to do their loving, had taken to using the local cemetery. He would take his amour up against a gravestone, and in this way they would find their mutual pleasure.

However, after a week or two the girl's back had become very painful, so she went to the doctor.

The doctor got her to strip, and examined her thoroughly.

"Well, doctor?" she asked, as she got dressed. "What's wrong with my back?"

"I don't know about your back," replied the doctor, "but your a**e died in 1904."

'You need to see a doctor about your condition, Roger.'

A man went to the doctor because he could not get an erection. Some weeks passed, but none of the treatments worked so finally the doctor gave him an ancient remedy which involved injecting him in his member. It was such a success that the man had a permanent erection, so he went back to the doctor to ask if it could be reduced.

"I'm sorry, it's impossible," said the doctor. "But surely you can do something. All drugs have antidotes."

"I agree," said the doctor, "but this injection wasn't a drug. Just three of sand to one of cement!"

A man goes to the doctor and tells him he swallowed three 10p pieces four weeks ago. "Can you get them out?" he asks.

The doctor looks at him, puzzled. "You swallowed the money four weeks ago and it's only now you're coming to see me?"

"That's right," replies the man. "I didn't need the money then."

A man goes to the doctor with a most unusual complaint. His penis is so big it drags his vocal chords down and causes him to stutter. The doctor tells him he can be cured, but it will mean an operation to take away eight inches from his very large member. The man agrees and the operation is a complete success.

However some weeks go by and the man misses his extra long penis — after all, it made him quite a celebrity. So he goes back to the doctor to ask if it can be put back on.

"S–s–s–orry," says the doctor, "that's not p–p–ppossible I'm aff–fraid."

A woman went to the doctor to tell him that every time she went to the toilet, pennies, ten-pence pieces and fifty-pence pieces came out.

"Don't worry," said the doctor. "You're just going through the change."

A buxom young lady goes to the doctor and he asks her to undress. When she's completely naked, he starts to feel her thighs.
"Do you know what I'm doing?" he asks.
"Yes, you're checking to see if there are any abnormalities."
Then he starts to fondle her breasts.
"Do you know what I'm doing now?"
"Yes, you're checking to see if there are any strange lumps."
Then the doctor lays her down on the table, jumps on top of her and starts making love.
"Now do you know what I'm doing?"
he asks.
"Yes," she replies. "You're catching herpes."

The old woman says to her next-door neighbour, who is suffering from piles, "Put some tea leaves up there. It's a good remedy."
The next-door neighbour does as she suggests, but the situation doesn't improve – in fact, it gets worse. So she goes to the doctor for a check-up.
As she's bending over, she says: "Can you see anything?"

The doctor replies, "No, but you're going to meet a tall, dark, handsome man on Monday."

A doctor is the only man who can get women to strip and then send their husbands the bill.

'I think he's swallowed the mobile phone.'

A man was asked to send a sample of his urine to the surgery before the doctor could complete his examination. Unfortunately, the man had to go to work, so asked the young boy next door to drop it in for him. On the way, however, the boy spilled most of it and, fearing trouble, topped it up with a cow's in a nearby field. It wasn't long before the doctor called for the man to come to the surgery as soon as possible. When he returned home later he was furious with his wife. "So much for all your fancy positions!" he snarled at her. "Now I'm pregnant, and it's all your fault!"

"I am very sorry to say that I have two bad pieces of news for you," said the doctor to his patient.
"Oh, dear, what are they?" asked the patient.
"You've been given only 24 hours to live," came the reply.
"Oh God, what other piece of bad news could there be?"
"I tried to get you on the phone all day yesterday."

A man goes to the doctor, upset because every night he has the same dream where two gorgeous women are trying to get into bed with him, but he keeps pushing them away.
The doctor asks what the man would like him to do and the patient replies, "Break both my arms."

A man went to the doctor and said he couldn't stop farting. It was dreadful – he just couldn't stop.
The doctor went away and came back with a huge long pole.
"Oh, no," said the man.
"It's all right," replied the doctor, "I'm only going to open the window."

Did you hear about the man who went to the chiropodist's and put his willy on the table?
When the chiropodist told him it wasn't a foot, he replied, "I know, but I'm proud it's 11 inches.""

The local mayor decided to do something useful for the community so went along to the sperm bank to make a donation.

"Have you been before?" asked the receptionist.

"I believe I have," replied the mayor. "You've probably got my notes from last time."

"Oh, yes," replied the girl. "You're going to need some help, so I'll put you in our category D area."

"Wait a minute, what do you mean category D? I don't need help!"

"I'm sorry, sir, but it says in your notes that you're a clueless w*nker."

A woman walked into the dentist very nervously and said, "I'd rather have a baby than have my teeth checked."

"OK," said the dentist, "that's fine, but I'll have to adjust the chair."

"It's no good, Mabel, I can't find anything wrong with you. It must be the effects of drinking," said the doctor.

"Well, in that case I'll come back when you're sober!" exclaimed the woman.

"Doctor, doctor, I'm so embarrassed. I've got several holes in my willy and when I go for a pee it sprinkles out all over me and over anyone standing nearby. Please say you can help."

The doctor considered the man for a few minutes and then wrote something down on a card.

"Here," he said, "take this card, on it is the name of a man who can help you."

"Oh, thanks, doc, will he be able to cure me?"

"No, but he's one of the country's finest flute players and he'll show you how to hold it properly."

I have a great doctor. If you can't afford the operation, he touches up the X-rays.

A man suffering from constipation was given a course of suppositories by his GP. But a week later he was back complaining they hadn't worked.
"Are you sure you've been taking them properly?"
"Of course I bloody well have," he answered angrily. "What do you think I've been doing, sticking them up my a**e?"

A very worried woman went to the doctor's to complain about the male hormone she was having to take.
"Oh, doctor, I'm growing hair in all sorts of places."
"Don't worry, that's not unusual in a case like this. Where in particular is the hair?"
"On my balls," she replied.

Doctor to woman patient: "You have acute appendicitis."
"Thank you, and you have a really nice bum," she replied.

A woman took her son to the doctor's because she was concerned that his penis was too small and not growing normally.

"Nothing to worry about," replied the doctor. "Every night, before he goes to bed, give him a cup of hot milk and stir in a teaspoon of this special B16 powder. That'll soon put things right."

A few evenings later, the little boy walked into the kitchen to find his mum putting three tablespoons of the powder into a mug of hot milk.

"But, Mum," said the boy, "the doctor only said a teaspoon."

"Oh, this isn't for you," she replied, "it's for your father."

"Every time I sneeze, I have an orgasm," said the girl to her doctor.

"What do you take for it?" he asked.

"Pepper."

A man is suffering very badly from severe headaches, dizziness and spots before the eyes.

"I'm sorry to say," said the doctor, "that you have got an infection in your testicles and unless you have them removed, the symptoms will spread."

Unwilling to accept this dreadful diagnosis, the man consults two other doctors, but they both give the same opinion. So, resigned to his fate, the man has both testicles removed.

Some days later, he decides to go shopping. "At least I can look good even if I don't feel it," he thinks to himself, so he visits the most exclusive gentlemen's outfitters for miles around.

"Ah, yes," says the tailor. "You're a 34in waist, 32in inside leg and 15in collar size."

"That's very impressive," says the man. "How can you tell?"

"Years of training, sir," replies the tailor. "I also know that you are a 40in

chest, take size 11 shoes and wear medium-sized underpants."

"Absolutely correct," says the astonished man, "except for the underpants. I take a small size."

"Then may I suggest you change the size, sir, otherwise you'll eventually start to suffer from severe headaches, dizziness and spots before the eyes."

'He was an optician.'

"I'm sorry, my glasses have broken again," said the man to the optician.
"Oh, dear," replied the optician. "It's becoming a bit of a habit. What happened this time?"
"Well, I was kissing my girlfriend when it happened."
"Really? I can't see why that should break your glasses."
"She crossed her legs," he replied.

A young couple were about to get married. The husband-to-be was ecstatic that such a gorgeous creature would want to marry such a boring old fart as himself. First they had to get the all clear from the doctor's. A few days after the examinations, the doctor asked the young man to come in for the results.
"Ah, Mr Brownall, do come in. I have some good news and some bad news."
"Oh, no," replied the poor man. "What's the bad news?"
"Your wife-to-be has herpes."
"Bloody hell!" he exclaimed. "What's the good news?"
"She didn't get it from you."

"Thanks for seeing us so quickly," said the grateful man to the dentist. "As I said on the phone, it's a bit of an emergency because this toothache's come just as we were flying out to the Bahamas at 6 o'clock tonight. Please take it out as quickly as possible. Don't worry about painkillers or anything like that, just yank it out."
"Well, I think I ought to warn you that it will be very painful if I don't use anything."
"Not to worry. Just get a move on."
"OK. I think you're very brave. Just pop up into the chair for me, please."
The man turned to his wife and said, "You heard what he said, Ruth, sit up in the chair."

"Oh, doctor," said the distraught patient. ***"Why do so many people take an instant dislike to me?"***
"Saves time," came the reply.

"I'm a little stiff from rugby, doctor."
"That's OK, it doesn't matter where you're from."

ON THE WARD

Three surgeons were relaxing in the bar after a conference and the first one said, "I had a pretty easy time last week. I had to operate on a computer analyst and when I opened him up, all the parts were filed and labelled and the retrieval system was very competent."

"Well, my week was even easier," said the second surgeon. "I had to operate on an electronics expert, all the different systems were colour-coded so you could see what was wrong immediately."

"Yes, that sounds good," said the third surgeon. "But I had the easiest of all. I had to operate on an estate agent. They've only got two moving parts – the mouth and the a**ehole – and they're both used for the same thing."

A young, rich lawyer had a very bad car crash. The car was a writeoff but even worse, the lawyer's arm had been severed. When the paramedics arrived, they heard him whimpering, "My BMW, oh no, my BMW!"

"Sir," said one of the helpers, "I think you should be more concerned about your arm."

The lawyer looked round and seeing just his shoulder, exclaimed,
"Oh no, my Rolex, my Rolex!"

A young nurse in nurses' home knocks on matron's door while she's having a bath.
"Yes, who is it?" asks the matron.
"I have Mr Thompson to see you."
"Come, come, nurse," responds matron. "I'm naked in the bath."
The nurse continues, "Mr Thompson, the blind man."
"OK, bring him in," says matron.
The door opens and the nurse and Mr Thompson enter the bathroom. Looking at the matron, Mr Thompson says, "Nice t*ts, matron. Now where do you want these blinds?"

A young nurse is walking along the corridor with one of her boobs hanging out of her uniform.
Matron appears and, on seeing this, is outraged. She asks for an immediate explanation. The nurse, with a resigned

air, replies, *"Sorry, Matron, it's these young house doctors. They never put anything back where they found it."*

A woman is visiting her sick aunt in hospital and, as she's leaving, she notices a ward completely enclosed by glass.
"Excuse me, nurse, what's that for?" she asks.
"That's the isolation ward. The man in there has got distemper, the plague, hepatitis and mumps."
As they look, they see a man going towards the glass, pushing a trolley.
"Is that his lunch?"
"Yes, he has Ryvita, After-eight chocolates and dried sheets of lasagne."
"Goodness, will that make him better?"
"No," replied the nurse, "but it's all we can slide under the door."

A man went into hospital to have a penis transplant, having lost his own in an industrial accident. After the operation, he immediately asked the surgeon how it went.

"Well," hesitated the surgeon, "mixed results really. The transplant was a success. I think you'll agree it's an impressive member, but unfortunately your hand has rejected it."

A rich young man, hearing about the amazing advances in body part transplants, decided he would like a new brain. He went to the specialist to find out what was on offer.

"Well, at the moment we have a computer analyst for £10,000; a university professor for £15,000 and a high court judge for £20,000."

"Money is no object," said the young man. "Tell me, what is the best and most expensive brain you have?"

"Well," said the specialist, "We do have an MP's on offer at £50,000."

"I don't understand," said the young man, "why is that one so much more expensive?"

"That's simple," said the specialist. "It's hardly ever been used."

A woman's face was very badly disfigured in
an accident.
"We can fix it," the surgeon said, "but it will cost you
£2,000 and we will need to take a skin graft from
another donor."
The woman's husband agreed to donate skin from his
backside, and the operation was a great success. His
wife was even more beautiful than she had been before
the accident. A few days later, the plastic surgeon rang
the husband to tell him he had paid £500 too much.
"Oh, no," said the husband, "it's worth it for the extra
pleasure I get everytime I see my mother-in-law kiss
my a**e."

*It was Monday morning and the great
but absent-minded rectal surgeon was
on his rounds.
Halfway round the ward, the nurse
nudged him and whispered: "Sir, you
have a suppository behind your
left ear."
"Oh, damn," cursed the surgeon. "That
means some bum's got my pencil."*

Two carrots were walking down the road one day when, all of a sudden, a car sped by out of control, and hit one of them.
The other carrot took him to the hospital where he had emergency surgery. After the operation, the surgeon approached the carrot in the waiting room. "I have good news and bad news. The good news is your friend will live. The bad news is he'll be a vegetable the rest of his life."

'I knew I was right. "The ankle bone's connected to the leg bone, the leg bone's connected to the..."'

DEAD FUNNY

It was Bob's funeral. His wife and three children were sitting in the front row listening to the vicar as he spoke enthusiastically about the man's life.
"He was a wonderful father, a hard-working man and a great asset to the community . . . "
At this point, the widow suddenly jumped up flustered and shooed her children out of the door, saying, "Oh dear, I think I must have got the wrong time. This can't be my Bob's funeral."

The devil tells a man who's just arrived in hell that he must choose one of three doors to enter, and in the room beyond he will spend eternity. The man is very worried that he will choose the wrong door so eventually persuades the devil to let him have a quick look behind the doors before making his choice.
Behind the first door he sees everyone standing on their head on a wooden floor. He doesn't fancy doing that for eternity, but the second door is even worse.

Everyone is standing on their head on a stone floor. However in the third room everyone is standing around drinking tea, ankle deep in manure. Oh well, thought the man, at least I'm not standing on my head, so he
tells the devil his choice is Room 3.
He goes into Room 3 and just as the door slams shut behind him he hears the devil shout out, "OK, everyone, tea break's over! Get back on your heads."

Two neighbours, one upright and a pillar of the church, the other a drinker and fornicator. Eventually the wicked one dies from his excesses, a few years later the other one dies, goes up to heaven and is astonished to see the wicked one with a large barrel of beer and a naked angel on his lap. The upright man is outraged and complains to St Peter.
"I denied myself all the good things in life so that I could come to heaven, and when I get here I see him enjoying himself when he should be in hell."
"Don't worry, he is in hell. The barrel's got a hole in it and the angel hasn't."

A woman returns from her husband's cremation and tips his ashes on to the kitchen table.

She then says to them, "You see this beautiful fur coat which I always asked for and never got. Well, I've bought it myself. And you see this pearl necklace I always longed for. Well, I've bought that too. And you see these exclusive leather boots, the ones I always wanted – I've bought them as well."

Then she stands up, leans over the table and blows her husband's ashes all over the floor, saying, "And there's that blow job you always wanted."

Two men, walking through a graveyard, stop to read the writing on one of the headstones which says, "Not dead, just sleeping".
One man turns to the other and says, "He ain't fooling nobody, only himself."

*"I'm sorry to hear you buried Jack yesterday," said the neighbour.
"Had to," replied Joan. "He was dead, you see."*

Three nuns at the Pearly Gates were being questioned by St Peter before being allowed to enter.
He said to the first nun, "Who was the first man?"
"Adam," she replied, the gates opened and in she went.
To the second nun he asked, "What was the name of the first woman?"
"Eve," came the reply and in she went.
Then to the third he said, "What were the first words spoken by Eve to Adam?"
"Wow, that's a hard one!" replied the nun and at that the gates opened and she disappeared inside.

*Did you hear about the woman who wore black garters?
To commemorate those who passed beyond.*

A new group of men had arrived in heaven and were told to get into two lines. One was for henpecked men, the other for independent, liberated men. However, only one man stood in this second line and, when asked why, he replied, "Because my wife told me I had to."

Two Scotsmen were talking in the pub and one turned to the other, saying, "Now, Mick, if I should die first, will you pour a bottle of the finest malt whisky over my grave?"
"That I will," said Jock, "but do you mind if it goes through my kidneys first?"

Two men arrive at the gates of heaven together and get asked some questions by the gatekeeper.
"Right, Mr White. I see from your records you've lived an exemplary life. You've done a lot for your community, been a good husband and a loving father. Just one question: have you ever been unfaithful?"
"Never," replied the man.
"In that case, I grant you a BMW and free petrol to get around heaven."

The gatekeeper then turned to the second man.
"Well, Mr Green. You've not had a bad life, you've been good to your parents, worked hard and lived modestly. One question: have you ever been unfaithful?"
Mr Green had to admit that he'd been unfaithful on four occasions.
"In that case, I grant you a mini for your transport around heaven."
A few days later the two men happened to meet up. Mr White was sitting dejectedly at the wheel of his car.
"What's wrong?" asked Mr Green. "You've got a lovely car, free petrol, why are you looking so miserable?"
Mr White replied sadly, "I've just seen my wife riding around on a bicycle."

At the funeral of his wife, Bob was distraught, his hands over his eyes, moaning and crying. The vicar thought he'd better go and comfort the poor man, so went over, put his arms around Bob's shoulders and said, "Come on, Bobby, time will help heal the loss and who knows, maybe one day you'll meet someone new." "So what?" cried Bob. "Where am I going to get a f*ck tonight?"

An estate agent named Bill Strange was making out his will and one of the instructions he put in was to have his gravestone inscribed with the words "Here lies a truthful man."

"But they won't know who it is," replied the lawyer.

"Oh, yes, they will," he smiled, "When people pass by and read the headstone they'll say, 'That's strange!' "

'Apparently, he believed in
reincarnation.'

Flo goes along to the local seance to try to get in touch with her late husband.

She's in luck and it's not long before she's asking him how he spends his time in heaven.

"Well, I get up in the morning, have something to eat, do a bit of bonking, take a nap, have something to eat, do a bit more bonking, go for a walk, eat, bonk, eat again and then go to bed," he said.

"But, Alf, you were never like that down here," said Flo, quite amazed.

"No, but I wasn't a rabbit then."

The two men had just reached the tenth hole when a funeral procession went slowly by. The first man stopped playing, took his hat off and bowed his head.

"That was very good of you," said the second man.

"Well, it's only right. We were married 27 years and she was a good wife to me," the first replied.

A man was lying on his death bed, time was running out and his family were standing round.

"Joe, Joe," whispered his wife, "is there anything I can do for you? Do you have a last wish?"

Joe lifted his head slowly from the pillow and sniffed the air.

He could smell his wife's baking in the oven.

"Can I have just a last slice of the wonderful cake you're baking?" he croaked.

"I'm afraid not, Joe, that's for the funeral."

It was the funeral of Big John Nowall, the most arrogant man in the district.

As his coffin passed into the church one of the spectators turned to the other and said, "I can't believe Big John's in there, the coffin looks so small."

"Oh, that's easy to explain," came the reply. "Once they let all the bullsh*t out of him, he fitted perfectly."

"Please come in and sit down, Mr Morton," said the doctor, looking grave. "I'm afraid your test results have come back and it's very bad news. You only have a year to live."

Mr Morton put his head in his hands and gasped, "Oh no, oh no, what shall I do?"

"Well, if I were you," replied the doctor, "I'd move out into the country, to a very quiet place, and marry an ugly, nagging woman. I can assure you, it'll be the longest year of your life."

Lying on his deathbed, the old man's eyes rested on the face of his sorrowful wife. "Dear Agnes," he rasped, "we've been through a lot together. When I was just 20, my parents were killed in a car accident and you were there for me. Then we had the terrible floods of '64 when we lost all our possessions and you helped me through it. Now I've caught this fatal disease and here you are by my side. Do you know," he continued with a spark of anger, "I'm beginning to think you're f*cking bad luck for me!"

An old woman had been going to the same doctor for over 50 years and during that time she had made his life a living hell by constantly complaining about one thing after another. Eventually, however, she died and was buried in the local churchyard, but it was less than a month later that the doctor also died and was buried in the plot next to her. For a few minutes after the mourners had gone all was quiet and then the doctor heard tapping on the side of his coffin.

"What is it now, Mrs Mowner?"
he sighed.

"Can you give me something for worms, doctor?"

A 'diddle' of antique dealers were tragically killed in a plane crash and the group of ten found themselves outside the Pearly Gates.

"Hm," said St Peter, scratching his head, "we don't usually let in so many antique dealers at the same time. I'll have to go and ask God."

St Peter went off and found God hard at work in his office.

"There's a group of antique dealers at the gates, shall we let them in?" he asked.

"Just this once," replied God. "If there are so many of them, they'll be too bothered about each other to cause havoc anywhere else."

St Peter went back to the entrance but returned moments later in a panic.

"They've gone!" he exclaimed breathlessly.

"What? The antique dealers?"

"No," replied Peter, "the Pearly Gates."

JUST PLAIN NUTS!

A therapist is trying to find out if there is any link between the number of times people have sex and the way they live their lives. He gathers together a group of people to survey.

"How many here have sex four times a week or more?" he asks of the group.

Half the class put their hands up.

"How many have sex four times a month?"

Ten hands go up.

"Four times a year?"

Two hands go up.

"And once a year?"

Up pops a hand at the back of the group, belonging to a man who is jumping up and down and smiling all over his face.

"Well," says the therapist, "you're very happy considering you only have sex once a year."

"I am!" he cries. "Tonight's the night!"

To assess Bob's state of mind the psychiatrist told him he was going to make some random marks on the paper

and Bob was to tell him what he saw. After the first mark Bob replied, "That's Madonna in the nude."
After the second mark he said, "That's my next-door neighbour stark naked."
After the third mark, "That's my wife's knitting circle with no clothes on."
The psychiatrist looked up exasperated. "The trouble with you, Bob, is that you're obsessed with sex."
"Get off!" retorted Bob angrily. "You're the one drawing the dirty pictures."

"What's up, Jack?" asked his mate.
"It's the wife. She introduced me to her psychiatrist this morning. She said, 'This is Jack, my husband, one of the men I was telling you about.' "

A man goes to the psychiatrist, who tells him, "You're mad."
The man says, "I want a second opinion."
"OK," answers the psychiatrist. "You're ugly too."

OLD AND IN THE WAY

The social worker was doing the rounds
at the local residential home and she
stopped to talk to Bob who was 92.
After she'd helped him to cut up his
food, she noticed a bowl of nuts on a
small table next to him.
"I was given them as a present," he
said, "but I don't like them much.
You're very welcome to have them."
Now the social worker was very fond of
nuts, so she nibbled away on them as
she continued to chat to old Bob. As
she was about to go she commented,
"Thanks for the nuts, but it's an odd
present to give to someone with
no teeth."
"Oh, no," he said. "When I was given
them, they had chocolate on."

An old man hobbled up to the ice-cream counter and asked for a chocolate cornet.
"Crushed nuts?" asked the salesgirl.
"No, arthritis," he replied.

Two old ladies are waiting at the bus stop when it begins to rain. The first woman, Doris, is smoking, so she takes a condom out of her bag, snips the end off and puts it over her cigarette to stop it getting wet.
"That's a great idea," enthuses Mabel, "I must do the same, where do you get them from?"
"Just pop into the chemist's," Doris replies.
So when they arrive in town, Mabel heads for the chemist shop and asks for a packet of condoms.
"What size would that be, madam?" enquires the assistant.
"I'm not sure," she replies, "One that fits a Camel, please."

A short-sighted woman was ill in bed and got a visit
from what she thought was the vicar. After he had
been with her for some time, he left as her
friend arrived.
"That was nice of the vicar to call, wasn't it?" said
the woman.
"No, dear, that was the doctor."
"Oh," she replied. "I thought the vicar was
very familiar."

*'Well, it doesn't look much like voluntary
euthanasia to me, Mrs Hill.'*

What does an 80-year-old woman have between her knees that a 20-year-old doesn't?
Her nipples.

A very old woman is walking down the lane when she sees a frog waving to her.

"Oh, Miss," he calls. "Please help me. If you give me a kiss I will turn into a handsome film star and I promise to stay with you forever."

The old woman picks up the frog and puts it straight into her handbag. "Hey!" shouts the frog. "Aren't you going to kiss me?"

"Oh, no," she replies. "When you get to my age, what good is a handsome man? A talking frog is much more exciting."

"Look, Flo," said the old woman, "they're selling three cucumbers for 60p."
"Well, I can always eat the other two," came the reply.

"I don't understand," said the young widow's friend. "You say your husband was killed by the bells. What does that mean?"

"Well, my husband was 75, and he would save up all his strength for us to make love on a Sunday to the rhythm of the church bells. He would still be here today if it hadn't been for that blasted ice-cream van going past."

An old man of 85 was sitting hunched up over his pint, crying his eyes out. "What's wrong?" asked a fellow drinker. "I got married two weeks ago to a beautiful curvaceous young redhead who's a gourmet cook, a wonderful conversationalist and fantastic in bed," replied the old man. "That's wonderful; you're a very lucky man. I don't understand why you're so upset." "I can't remember where I live!" he cried.

An old lady went to the doctor complaining of
constipation. "I sit there for hours," she said.
"Ah, yes, but do you take anything?" asked the doctor.
"Oh, yes, I take my knitting."

*"Are you sure it's a good idea to marry
such a young, energetic girl?"
said the doctor to his elderly patient.
"You know, such energetic sex could
prove fatal."
"Oh well," said the old man, "if she
dies, at least she dies happy."*

It's good to exercise. My grandpa started walking five
miles a day when he was 60. Today he's 95 and we
don't know where the hell he is.

*What is the similarity between men and
old age?
They both come too soon.*

A rich old man of 88 married a beautiful young girl of 23 and it wasn't long before she was expecting a baby. Overjoyed at the news, the old man was taken aside by his kindly doctor, who had known his patient for a long time and was concerned for his well-being.

"Listen, Jack, it's about the baby. Let's see if I can explain what I mean. There was a big game hunter who'd spent all his life in Africa, but was now really too old to last the distance. He decided to go out one last time, but being so absentminded, instead of his gun, he took his walking stick with him. Time went by, when suddenly a man-eating lion confronted the man. He lifted his stick and shot the animal dead."

"But, that can't be!" cried his patient. "Someone else must have shot it."

"Absolutely," replied the doctor. "That's what I'm trying to tell you."

A retired colonel was invited to a reunion dinner and halfway through the proceedings he rang his wife.
"Agnes, this reunion is turning out to be more than I bargained for. They've got lots of naked girls dancing on the table and they're giving their favours to

anyone who's interested. What do you think I should do?"
She replied, "If you think you can do anything you'd better get home straightaway."

Two old women were catching up on the local gossip. "I see old Violet Henshaw has just cremated her third husband," said one.
"So I see," replied the other. "Some of us can't get a husband at all, and Violet's got husbands to burn!"

The old couple went to Eastbourne for their two-week summer holiday, but, alas, the day before they were due to return Maurice collapsed and died. The funeral took place a few days later. As friends and relatives filed past his coffin, Rose turned to the widow and remarked, "Gosh, Ethel, he looks wonderful."
"Oh, yes," agreed Ethel, "those two weeks in Eastbourne did him a power of good."

Two old men were sitting on the beach watching the bikini-clad girls walking by, running into the water and playing beach volleyball.
"Do you think all this exercise keeps you fit?"
asked one.
"I should say so," replied the other. "I walk two miles every day just to watch this."

A very old man would take his daily walk around the garden and that would be the most exercise he could manage before collapsing in his well-worn armchair for the rest of the day. One morning he was halfway round on his regular stroll when, to his surprise, he found an old golden idol sticking out of the bushes.
"Goodness me, what have we here?"
he murmured and, to his further astonishment, the idol spoke back.
"Please help me," it said. "I'm not really an idol, I'm a beautiful young girl, but many years ago a spell was put on me and it can only be broken if I have sex with a man."

"Oh, no," said the man. "I can't manage that sort of thing any more."

She begged him again, "Oh please, please help me. I've been lost in this undergrowth for years it may be such a long time before another man finds me."

The man thought for a moment.

"OK," he replied, "I've got an idea. I'll just go and call my son, he's an idle f*cking b*stard."

'Hi, Mum. It's bad news: he's got the all clear.'

PENALTY AREA

This Glasgow Celtic fan was such a fanatic even the house was painted green and white.
His wife said, "I'm p*ssed off, you think more of Celtic than you do of me."
"Christ Almighty, woman," he said. "I think more of f*cking Rangers than I do you."

Two rival football supporters travelled home from the match in the same railway compartment. As Tony got up to go to the buffet car, he asked the other if he could get him anything.
"Thanks, mate," replied the man. "A glass of lager please."
When Tony had gone, the rival fan gobbed in Tony's football cap which was lying on the seat. Then Tony returned and handed over the glass of lager, which his rival drank down greedily.
At last it was Tony's stop and as he got up to leave, he put his cap on and immediately realized what had happened.
*"You know, mate," he said looking at the smirk on the other's face, "we really should stop doing all this – gobbing in caps and p*ssing in lager."*

A professional footballer was out on a first date and after the pubs closed he invited her back to his place. Removing his jacket, she noticed UMBRO tattooed on both arms and he explained it was part of an advertising campaign – he received £1,000 for each arm. When he saw how impressed she was he removed his shirt and there across his chest was the word PUMA.

"I got £1,500 for this," he said. "And £800 each for these," and he dropped his trousers to show the word KAPPA tattooed on both ankles.

"But this is the best," he laughed, and with that he showed her his penis.

"Oh!" she exclaimed. "Why SLAG?"

"No, no," he replied, "I got £8,000 for this and if you stick around a while you'll see it says SLAZENGER."

"Football, football, football! I'm sick of it. If you took me out on Saturday afternoon instead of going to the match I think I'd die of shock."
"Now, now, dear," said her husband.
"It's no good trying to bribe me."

It was the women's football league final and a large crowd had turned out to watch. But ten minutes into the game, the goalkeeper was thrown against the post and knocked to the ground. Immediately, all the linesmen and officials rushed over to help her, but after five minutes and no sign of recovery, the referee walked over to find out what was going on.
"We're trying to give her the kiss of life," explained one of the officials, "but she keeps trying to get up and walk away."

'Run, they lost again.'

"Now, listen, son, we can't afford for you to get injured before the cup match next week, so I'll put you on for the first 45 minutes and pull you off at half-time."
"Wow, thank, boss, all I got at my old club was a slice of orange at half-time."

While David Beckham is hanging around in a department store one day, waiting for Posh to finish trying on frocks, he wanders into the kitchen department, and sees a cylindrical metal object which he finds very intriguing.
"What's this?" he asks the assistant.
"It's a Thermos flask," she replies.
"But what does it do?" asks the Boy Wonder.
"It keeps hot things hot, and cold things cold," the assistant tells him.
Thinking this is marvellous, David buys one, and takes it to training with him next day.
"Look what I've got," he tells the lads, proudly. "It's a Thermos flask."
The lads are impressed. "What does it do?" they ask.
"It keeps hot things hot and cold things cold," replies David.
"And what have you got in it?" asks Gary Neville.
"Two cups of coffee and a choc ice," says David.

A famous footballer was asked if he would appear nude in a glossy magazine. "We'd like you to pose holding a ball," explained the editor. "OK, but what do I do with my other hand?"

Two football fans were down at the front of the crowd when some hooligans towards the back started to throw beer cans.
One of the fans got very agitated and couldn't concentrate on the game properly.
"Don't worry," said his mate. "It's like the war, if it's got your name on it . . . "
"That's the trouble," interrupted the other. "My name's Foster."

*Which three league teams have swear words in their names?
Arsenal, Scunthorpe and Manchester f*cking United.*

A Plymouth Argyle fan is walking through the park one day when he stumbles over an old lamp. A genie pops out and tells him he has just one wish, what would he like. The man looks down at his dog and tells the genie he would like his dog to win the Crufts Dog Show to become supreme champion.

"You've got to be joking!" replies the genie. "Just look at him. He must be on his last legs, he's a flea-bitten old mongrel with half a tail."

"OK," sighs the man, "in that case can you make Plymouth win the FA Cup?"

The genie looks at him for a moment and then says, "Let's have another look at this dog then."

A footballer got kicked in his vital parts and lay doubled up on the ground, holding himself and moaning.

"Are you alright, mate?" asked the first-aid man, rushing up to him.

"For God's sake," groaned the man, "don't worry about rubbing them, just count them!"

A motorist is stopped for going through a red light and is asked to take a breathalyzer test.

"I can't blow," says the man. "I suffer from asthma," and he shows the policeman his asthmatic's card.

"OK, then we'll have to take you down to the station for a blood test."

"I can't. I'm a haemophiliac," and he produces a doctor's note.

"In that case, it'll have to be a urine test."

Once again, the man produces a card from his wallet. It reads "Manchester City Supporters Club – please don't take the p*ss".

'Shall I sign it in joined-up writing?'

Coventry City suffered a break-in recently when thieves stole the entire contents of the trophy room. Police are looking for a man carrying a roll of sky-blue carpet.

A man walks into the local pub with a parrot on his shoulder to watch Wales v. Albania on TV. The match soon starts to go Albania's way and, after ten minutes, they score. All of a sudden, the parrot starts to make awful moaning noises.

"Sorry," says the man, "he's a fanatical Wales supporter, so he's obviously quite upset."

The score remains the same until half-time, but Albania score a second goal only five minutes into the second half. This time the parrot is beside himself with anguish – moaning, stomping up and down and burying his head in his feathers. When a third Albanian goal is scored, there's absolute chaos. The bird starts pulling out all his feathers until there is a pile of them on the floor.

"Jesus!" says the barman, "if he reacts like this when they lose, what's he like when they win?"

"I don't know, I've only had him a few years."

GOLF CRAZY

Angry wife to husband: "You were twice as long on the golf course today. Why's that?"

"A slight problem," replied the husband. "Old Jack died on the ninth hole and from then on in it was play the hole, drag Jack, play the hole, drag Jack, play the hole . . . "

'Sorry, won't be a minute.'

An Englishman, a Scotsman and an Arab were talking about their families.

"I have ten children," said the Englishman. "One more, and I'll have my own football team."

"I have 14 children. One more, and I'll have my own rugby team," replied the Scotsman.

"Well, I have 17 wives," said the Arab. "One more and I'll have my own golf course.""

For more than six months a woman had been having golf lessons but still couldn't hit the ball more than a few yards down the fairway.

Unable to take it any longer, her coach shouted, "You're not holding the club properly! Hold it like you hold your husband's c*ck!"

So the woman did and the ball flew through the air, landing on the green.

"That's terrific," said the stunned coach. "You can take the club out of your mouth now."

A golfer was returning to the clubhouse after a disastrous day on the course. He'd been over par on every hole, lost three balls, and eventually thrown away most of his clubs in a fury.

As he stamped up to the clubhouse, he stood on a rake and yelled, "That was the best two balls I've hit today."

A young couple meet on holiday and, after a whirlwind romance, decide to get married.

"I must warn you," says the man, "that I'm golf crazy. I like to play every day, you'll hardly ever see me."

"Don't worry," she says. "I have something to confess as well. I'm a hooker."

"That's OK," he says. "You're probably not keeping your wrists straight."

It was competition day at the local golf club and the retired colonel found himself paired up with the bishop.

They set off and it wasn't long before the colonel,

missing a short putt, exclaimed, "Sh*t! Missed the b*stard!"

The bishop shook his head reproachfully.

A little later, the same happened again, and the colonel missed an easy putt.

"Sh*t! Missed the b*stard!" he shouted loudly, at which point the bishop was forced to tell him that the Almighty would not be pleased with his language and that something dreadful might happen to him.

But almost immediately on the next hole, the colonel missed his drive and was so incensed he shouted and swore for a good half minute.

All of a sudden the skies opened, there was a terrible clap of thunder, and lightning struck the bishop dead.

After a short pause, a voice was heard from above, "Sh*t! Missed the b*stard!"

Each week the vicar and a retired colonel played a round of golf and, no matter how well he did, the vicar was never able to beat him. After one very close defeat the colonel turned to him and said, "Don't worry, Vicar, you win in the end. You'll be burying me in the not

too distant future."
"That's true," said the vicar dispiritedly.
"But even then it'll be your hole."

A group of men, very competitive when it came to golf, were arguing on the ninth tee. When the captain arrived and asked what was wrong they replied, "See my partner, Bob, over there, lying in the bunker? He's just died of a stroke and these buggers want to add it to my score."

It's the honeymoon night and the happy couple strip off as quickly as possible and jump into bed. But she whispers to him, "Before we start, I feel I must tell you that one of my previous lovers was the captain of our local golf club."
"Listen, love," he replies. "Whatever went on before doesn't matter; we're married now, and nothing will come between us."
For the next 30 minutes they make love.
Afterwards the husband picks up the phone.
"What are you doing?" she asks.
"I'm going to get us some smoked salmon

and pink champagne," he says, smiling.

"Oh, no," she says, "the captain of the golf club would have made love to me again."

So once again they have 30 minutes of unbridled passion and then once again he calls for room service.

"No, no," she cries, "he would have done it a third time."

Again, they do it but by this time the husband is exhausted.

He reaches for the phone and before she can say anything, he says wearily, "I'm just ringing the golf captain to find out what the par for the hole is."

'I think my husband suspects.'

"Molly, would you get married again if I died?" asked her husband.

"Probably," she replied.

"And would you share with him all the little things we did together?"

"I expect so," she said.

"And would you let him have my prize golf clubs?"

"Oh, no," she replied, "he's left-handed."

A local golf club was being built for the less well-off in the district and it was agreed that the women's team would practise once the men had finished and they would share the same equipment. That night, once the men had gone, the ladies walked out to the first hole when there was a sudden yell.

"Hold on," shouted Doreen. "I've got the clubs, but the men have gone home and taken their balls with them!"

An old man knocked at the door of the solicitors' offices and asked one of the partners if his grandson, an articled clerk, could have the afternoon off to accompany him to the last day of the Open at Wentworth.

"I'm afraid you're out of luck. He's taken the afternoon off to go to your funeral," came the reply."

For a whole week, the golfing instructor has been giving lessons to a new female member of the club and at the end of the session he invites her out for a drink. She accepts and they go off into town. After a couple of drinks, he invites her to dinner, then to a club and finally back to his place.

"Look, Ron," she says as they sit on his sofa, "I think I ought to tell you that I'm not really a woman, I'm a transvestite."

"Why, you awful, you . . . immoral . . . "

"Come on, Ron, we are living in a more tolerant society."

"But it's unforgivable. You've been playing off the women's tee all week!"

On his tour of the world's best golf courses, a man ends up on a course in Africa. As he sets off for the first hole, he is accompanied by a caddie who carries a shotgun.

"Surely we don't need that," he says.

"Believe me, we do," replies the caddie.

All goes well until they get to the seventh hole and the man's tee shot lands in the bunker. As he steps into the sand a huge cobra suddenly looms up and, as quick as a flash, the caddie aims his gun and shoots the snake dead.

"Bloody hell, I see what you mean," says the golfer, sweating profusely.

Then at the 12th hole, the ball lands in the rough and, as the golfer goes over to hit it, a lion appears unexpectedly.

Again, the caddie immediately takes aim and frightens the lion off with a gun blast. The rest of the holes are played without interruption, but on the 18th the golfer finds he's hit the ball close to the water. As he steps up to take the shot a crocodile rears up out of the lake and grabs hold of him.

"Quick, man, do something!" he yells at the caddie.

"Sorry, sir, I can't give you a shot at this hole."

Two inexperienced lady golfers were teeing off on the seventh hole when the second player's shot went so wide it hit a man on the eighth tee. He immediately clasped his hands to his crotch in sheer agony as he fell to the ground.
"Oh, I'm so very sorry," said the woman as she ran over to help him. "Is there anything I can do? I'm a masseuse so I might be able to ease the pain."
With that, she ordered the man to lie on the ground with his hands by his side. She then undid his trousers and started to massage his manhood.
"There, is that helping?" she asked looking very concerned.
"That's great," he replied, "but my finger is still throbbing."

"My doctor has told me I must give up golf."
"Oh, I see he's played with you too!"

"What's wrong, Beryl?" asked Joan, seeing her friend in floods of tears. "It's Jack, he's left me." "Oh, get away, he's always walking out on you." "You don't understand. This time it's for good, he's taken his golf clubs."

Violet had been moaning at Jack for ages because he wouldn't teach her golf. Eventually it got him down so much he gave in and took her out one Monday afternoon. After spending some time discussing the

'You should involve your wife more in golf like I did, Martin. . . . Come on, dear, keep up.'

finer points of the game, they stepped up to the first tee and Violet hit a mighty drive which landed straight on the green and disappeared into the hole.

"OK," said Jack, "I'll take a practice shot now, and then we'll begin."

The men were talking in the clubhouse bar after spending a day on the greens. Each was recounting his golfing experiences.

One said, "If I'm going round on my own, the dog comes to keep me company and if I go one over par on a hole he somersaults backwards."

"That's incredible!" responded the others.

Warming to the subject, the man continued. "And if I go two over par at a hole, he does a double somersault backwards."

"Amazing," came the response, "that's quite a feat, how does he do it?"

"Oh, I kick him twice."

HOWZAT!

Three cricket managers meet up to talk over the previous cricket season and as they are strolling back to their hotel they notice a sign saying, "Come and find out what the future has in store for you – speak to Mystic May now." They've had a bit to drink, so decide to go in and have some fun.

"We'd like to know if God's a cricket fan and, if so, can he tell us how our teams will do in the future?" says one of them, winking at the other two.

But Mystic May takes them very seriously and asks them which teams they manage and what they want to ask.

The first says, "When will Somerset win a major trophy?"

After a moment's silence, a loud voice is heard: "2040."

"Damn, I'll have gone by then."

The second man asks the same question for Lancashire and the voice says, "2038."

"Oh, no, I won't be here either."

Then the third man, one of the England Selectors, asks, "When will England next win the Ashes?"

This time, there is an even longer silence before the voice booms out.

"Bloody hell, I won't be around either."

A man found himself hurtling to earth after his parachute failed to open. Thinking this was the end, he was suddenly amazed to see a group of men standing in a circle below, shouting up to him, "Don't worry, you'll be all right, we'll catch you!" Unable to believe his luck, he was just about to relax when, looking down again, he realized they were the English cricket team.

A very famous cricketer who could play right-handed or left-handed was asked how he decided which way to play that day. The man explained.
"If my wife is lying on her left side, I play left-handed and if she's lying on her right side, then I play right-handed."
"Ah, but what if she's lying on her back?"
"In that case, I ring up and tell them I'll be late that morning."

A passer-by happened to see a coffin being brought out of the church, with a cricket bat and pads on its lid. He turned to one of the mourners and said, "Like his cricket, did he?"
"Still does," replied the mourner. "He's straight off to a match after this, once they've buried his wife."

The finest batsman the county ever had was killed in a bad car crash and one of the substitute cricketers thought it was time he showed what he could do.
"Listen, boss, how about me taking his place?" he asked.
"Well, I'm not sure," replied the manager. "We'll have to see what the undertakers say first."

He was the laziest boy in the class. Only yesterday, the children were asked to produce an account of a cricket match. All the others spent an hour writing while he took 30 seconds. When the teacher saw it later she read, "Rain stopped play."

A horse was walking by the village green when he spotted a game of cricket in progress. He went over to the captain and asked, "Any chance of a game?" The captain was dumbfounded when he heard the horse talk, but it so happened that one of his team had just retired injured so he agreed to put him in at number 7. The horse was sensational. He hit a four or a six off every ball in the over and the crowd were going wild. However, when the bowler changed ends, batsman 6 hit a single.

"Run," he shouted to the horse, "run, quick." But the horse didn't move an inch and the batsman was run out.

"Why didn't you run?" the batsman demanded, as he left the field.

"Listen," said the horse angrily. "If I could run I'd be at the racecourse now, not stuck in some bloody village cricket team."

Why did the battered wife decide to live with the English cricket team?
They don't beat anybody.

AWAY GAMES

A world-class gymnast, away from home at an
athletics meeting, spends a night of passion with
one of her fellow athletes. On returning home she's
overcome with guilt and goes off to confession.
When the priest gives her absolution she's so relieved
she comes out of church doing handstands and double
somersaults just as Mrs O'Neill is going in.
"Oh, no," murmurs the woman. "What a day to do that
as the penance – and me with no knickers on."

'I told you not to shout abuse.'

The local tennis club was having its annual competition and Steve had just beaten Malcolm, a notoriously bad loser. In the bar afterwards, Malcolm passed Steve and, running his hand over Steve's bald head, remarked, "My goodness, your head feels just like my wife's backside."

Quick as a flash, Steve stroked his head and replied, "Well I never, it does, doesn't it?"

Jack had just played a gruelling game of tennis down at his local club when he looked at his watch and realized he was going to be late for his mother's cocktail party.

"Damn," he muttered to himself as he hastily changed and rushed off home, forgetting about the two tennis balls that he'd put in his pocket.

In fact he didn't realize anything was wrong until he started getting odd looks from a lovely young girl. Blushing, he said, "Oh, they're just my tennis balls."

"Golly," she replied. "I bet that's even more painful than tennis elbow."

SHORT ORDERS

Why don't blind men skydive?
Because it scares the sh*t out of the dog.

Girls, what can you do to be sure you get something hard between your legs? Buy a motorbike.

What's the definition of obscenity?
Anything that gives the judge an erection.

"No, no, no," exclaimed the female centipede, crossing her legs, "a thousand times, no."

Did you hear about the man whose mistress kept demanding very expensive presents?
He ended up having to marry her for his money.

Having feasted magnificently on a stray bull, the lion roared with satisfaction. However, the sound carried to a group of hunters who tracked him down and shot him.
So please beware: if you're full of bull, keep your mouth shut.

You know you're getting old when you have a party and the neighbours don't complain.

'Erm, we're just checking. You are in fancy dress, aren't you?'

PUB CRAWL

A man goes into a bar with a cat and a heron and orders two pints of beer for himself and the cat, and a glass of wine for the heron.

"That'll be £4.20," says the barmaid.

"You get these, heron," says the cat, so the bird pays.

A little later, they order another round and this time the cat says to the man, "Your round, mate," so the man pays up.

The three stay at the bar all night drinking heavily, but never once does the cat pay for a round, always having some excuse. Eventually, the bemused landlord cannot contain his curiosity any longer and asks the man what he's doing with the cat and heron.

"Well," says the man, "my fairy godmother appeared to me last week, and told me she would grant me one wish. I think she must have *been having a bit of a joke with me, though, because this wasn't what I had in mind when I asked for a tall bird with a tight pussy."*

☞ ★ ☜

The man staggered into the bar and shouted, "A double whisky bartender, and a drink for all your customers . . . and have one yourself."

"Well, thank you, sir."

Moments later, the man shouted again, "Another drink all round and one for yourself, bartender."

"Excuse me, sir, but I think you ought to pay for the other round first."

"But I haven't got any money."

The bartender was beside himself with rage.

"Then f*ck off and don't even think about showing your face here again!" he roared.

However, ten minutes later, the man reappeared, and once more staggered to the bar.

"Double whisky," he slurred, "and a drink for all my friends."

"I suppose you'll be offering me a drink as well," growled the bartender sarcastically.

"Oh, no," replied the man, "you get nasty when you drink."

The man stormed into the bar and yelled, "OK, you b*stards, which prat just painted the back of my car pink?" From the corner, a huge Hell's Angel stood up and growled, "I did. You got a problem with that?"

"No, no," stuttered the man. "I just thought you'd like to know, the first coat is dry."

An Englishman, an Irishman and a Scotsman walked into a bar and each ordered a pint of beer.

However, when the drinks arrived, all three pints had a fly swimming around in the froth.

The Englishman looked at it in disgust and pushed it away.

The Irishman picked the fly out with his fingers, threw it on the floor, then drank the beer.

The Scotsman also picked the fly out of the froth, then began shaking it over the top of the pint, saying, "Spit it out now, y'little b*stard!"

A drunk staggers into a bar and spots a man drinking in the corner. He goes up to him and says at the top of his voice, "I've just sh*gged your mum, it was great."

There's a hushed silence as everyone waits to see a reaction, but the man ignores the comment and the drunk wanders away. But ten minutes later he shouts at him again from the other end of the bar, "And I'll tell you now, your mum's the best lay for miles."

Again, everyone waits with bated breath but nothing happens. They all return to their drinks, but by now the drunk can't leave it alone.

He staggers over to the man once more and yells, "And another thing, she says she wants it from me every night!"

Sighing audibly, the man puts down his beer and places his hand on the drunk's shoulder.

"Just go home Dad, you've had enough."

A man walks into a pub and is greeted by a crocodile.
"What'll it be?" asks the crocodile.
The man just stares at him open-mouthed.
"Come on," he says, "haven't you seen a
crocodile before?"
"Oh, sorry," he stutters, "it's just that I never thought
the horse would sell this place."

'Don't worry, he always feigns death when it's
his round.'

Every day a man in the local bar would be surrounded by beautiful women – like bees round a honey pot.
"I don't understand it," said the barman. "It's not as if he has a lot of money or dresses expensively.
All he does is just sit there licking his eyebrows."

A man walked into a bar with a tiny pianist on his shoulder.
The pianist could only have been a foot tall. During the evening the pianist entertained the customers with his brilliant playing and eventually the barman asked the man where he got this wonderful entertainer.
"Well, I was walking in a wood and came across an old bottle. In the bottle was a genie who offered me anything I wanted, but I think she was a little hard of hearing, because I didn't ask for a twelve-inch pianist."

What a landlord! I asked him for something cold, tall and full of gin and he introduced me to his wife.

A man thought up a clever way to make some money. His friend had an unusual anatomy in that he had three balls.

"We can make a fortune," the first man told him. "Come on, I'll show you."

They went into the local pub and the man got everyone's attention by standing on a chair and shouting, "I'll bet anyone in this bar that my friend and the barman there have five balls between them."

People rushed forward and soon a lot of money had changed hands. At that point, the man turned to the barman and said,

"I hope you don't mind taking part in this bet."

"Not at all," replied the barman. "It's amazing to find a man with four balls to go with my one."

A man is trying to decide what to call his new bar when he spots Lisa coming up the street. Now this man is really keen on Lisa, who's not only gorgeous but has legs that go on for ever. That's it, he thinks, I'll call my new bar Lisa's Legs.

The next day three men are waiting outside the bar when a cop stops to ask them what they are doing.
"We're waiting for Lisa's Legs to open so we can go in and satisfy ourselves,"
they reply.

I saw this white horse standing behind a bar.
I said, "Do you know there's a whisky named after you?"
He said, "What – Adrian?"

A giant of a man, very drunk and very mean, throws open the doors of the pub and shouts loudly, "All you on the right side are c*cksuckers and all you on the left are motherf*ckers!"
Suddenly a man runs from left to right.
"Where are you going, wimp?" roars the drunk.
"Sorry, sir, I was on the wrong side,"
he replies.

After gulping down a Scotch in the local bar, the man bets the bartender £50 he can p*ss in the empty glass. Eager to make some easy money, the bartender agrees, so the man drops his trousers and starts to p*ss everywhere – on the floor, the bar, the tables, even the bartender himself. But nothing goes in the glass. The bartender chuckles to himself and demands the £50.

"Just a second," replies the man. He goes up to two guys sitting in the corner and comes back moments later with £200 in his hand.

"Here's your £50," he says, and hands over the money.

Puzzled, the bartender asks, "What was all that about?"

"Well, you see, I bet them £200 that I could p*ss all over this pub, and over you, and you'd still be smiling at the end of it."

Jack was sitting at the bar gazing dejectedly into his beer.
"What's up?" asked the barman.
"It was last night," he replied. "I got so drunk I don't remember what I did, but when I saw a woman in bed with me I naturally gave her £50."
"Well, that's reasonable, even if you don't remember it," said the barman.

"It's not that," said Jack. "It's the fact that it was my wife and she automatically gave me £10 change."

"If you don't keep the noise down, I'm going to have to arrest you," advised the policeman to the drunk who was staggering down the road singing at the top of his voice.

"Oh, have a heart, officer," slurred the man, "it's the works' outing."

The policeman looked round him. "Where are the others then?"

"There aren't any others," he replied. "I'm self-employed."

A man walks up to the bar and asks for an entendre.

"Would you like a single or a double?" asks the barmaid.

"A double please," he replies.

"OK, sir, so yours is a large one."

A man walked into the pub with a dog.

"I'm sorry, sir, no dogs allowed in here."

"Yes, but he's a really intelligent dog, ask him to do anything and he will."

"OK," said the barman. "Tell him to go and get me a newspaper."

The man hands the dog £5 and off he goes. Two hours go by and there's still no sign of the dog, so the anxious owner goes looking for him. After roaming the streets, shouting his name, he eventually finds him mating with a bitch in an alley.

"What's all this about?" asked the owner. "You've never done this before."

"No, but I've never had so much money before," replied the dog.

A bloke goes into a pub and orders a triple whisky and a pint of beer. As soon as the barman puts them in front of him he drinks them all down in one gulp.

"I shouldn't be drinking all this," he says.

"Why's that?"
"Because I've only got 20p on me."

An anti-drink campaigner walks into a local bar and calls for the customers' attention.

"I would like to show you all something about drinking," he announces and at that point he puts two jars on the table. One he fills with whisky, the other with water. Then he produces two earthworms and drops one into each jar. The one in the whisky jar breathes his last and sinks to the bottom while the other swims happily around in the water.

"So what does this show you about drinking?" asks the campaigner.

A voice at the back replies, "If you drink, you won't have worms!"

A man walks into a bar with a toy poodle on a lead.
"No dogs allowed in here," says the barman. "Only guide dogs for the blind."

"But I am blind," insists the man.
"Well, that's not a guide dog."
"Why, what is it?"
"It's a poodle."
"Bugger, I've been conned."

A man goes into a pub carrying an octopus.
"Sorry, mate, you can't bring that in here," says
the barman.
"Hold on a minute," says the man, "this isn't just any
old octopus. This one can play every single musical
instrument you care to put before him. How about a
small wager? If he can play all the instruments you can
produce, I get free drinks for the night. If not, then I'll
buy everyone in here a drink."
The barman agrees and the wager begins. First, the
octopus plays the piano, then it plays the trumpet –
a superb piece of jazz – followed by the double bass,
violin and harp.
"I'm not beaten yet!" thinks the barman.
He goes upstairs into the attic and finds his old

bagpipes. They haven't been played for years, but he dusts them down and hands them to the octopus. The octopus looks at them, feels them, but doesn't start to play.

"Gotcha," smiles the barman triumphantly. "Time to pay up."

"Just a moment," replies the man confidently. "When he realizes he can't f*ck it, then he'll play it."

'I killed my wife and buried her in the garden today. . . Does that make me a bad person, Joe?'

A man walks into a pub and orders a pint of beer and a pasty.
"How much will that be?" he asks.
"Nothing, sir, it's on the house."
A little later, the man orders another beer and again is told it's on the house. After a third pint, he asks the barman:
"Why are all the drinks free today?"
"Oh, it's quite simple," replies the barman. "The owner of this pub doesn't know that I know he's upstairs with my wife. So I'm doing to him down here what he's doing to me up there."

A man walks into a pub, orders a pint of beer and asks the barman if he can borrow the pub's newspaper to do the crossword.

The barman thinks for a moment and then replies, "I'd just like to ask you a couple of questions first. Tell me, when a sheep dumps, why does it come out in little dottles?"

The man shook his head. "I don't know."

"OK," said the barman. "What about cows, why does it come out in a round 'pat'?"

Again the man shook his head.
"Listen, mate," said the barman scornfully. "You don't know sh*t, so I don't reckon you'll be able to do this crossword!"

Two mates were talking over a pint of beer.
"What's wrong, Jack? You don't look so good," said Bob.
"It's this bloody toothache, been driving me mad, I just can't get rid of it."
"Well, maybe I can help you there. I had a toothache a couple of months ago and, believe it or not, my wife gave me a blow job and I was cured. Why don't you try it?"
"Thanks, Jack, I'll have a go. Will your wife be home tonight?"

A man walks into a bar with a Cornish pasty on his head and asks the barman for a pint of beer. Unable to conceal his curiosity the barman hands the man the beer and says, "Excuse me, sir, I couldn't help but notice that you have a Cornish pasty on your head." "That's right," replies the man. "I always have a Cornish pasty on my head on a Thursday."
"But, sir, it's Friday today."
"Oh, no," says the man. "I must look a right prat."

A man went into a bar and ordered a gin and tonic. When it was placed before him, he exclaimed, "Hey, an ice cube with a hole in it, that's new!"
"No, it isn't," commented a sullen-looking man sitting next to him.
"I married one."

One Saturday lunchtime at the pub, Martin spots Kevin over the other side of the bar.
"Hello, Kevin, been away? Haven't seen you for a while."
"Oh, hello, Martin. As a matter of fact I have. I went on a weekend course to that big hotel off the A1. It was all

about reincarnation. Very good. Mind, it cost £400."
"Phew! That's a bit steep."
"Yes, I suppose it was. Still, you only live once."

A man spends the evening in the pub and by the end of the night he's so drunk he can hardly walk home. But he sets off and in a befuddled haze decides to take a shortcut through the park and climb over the wall. All goes well until the final gate which is topped by sharp glass, and while shinning over this he badly rips his backside.

By the time he gets home, he's in agony, so, quietly, without waking the wife, he heads for the bathroom to inspect the damage, clean up the wounds and do a bit of safety first. The next morning he crawls out of bed with a king-sized hangover and an aching a**e.

"What did you get up to last night?" accused his wife. "You were well p*ssed when you got in last night."

"No, I wasn't," he replied. "What makes you think that?"

"I'll tell you. I found all our plasters on the bathroom mirror this morning," she retorted.

☞ ★ ☜

Two men were chatting over a pint.
Bob turns to John and says, "You're looking down, what's wrong?"
"It's the wife, since she's started this high-powered job she's cut our sex down to three times a week."
"You're lucky," remarked Bob. "She's cut me out completely."

☞ ★ ☜

"I'm fed up, Steve," sighed his mate, *Jack. "Bloody sex, it's a minefield. If you go out with girls you might get some sort of STD. If you go out with boys, you could get AIDS. In fact, you can't even go out with yourself any more for fear of getting RSI."*

☞ ★ ☜

A fire engine came racing around the corner and disappeared up the road, bells clanging wildly.

As it passed The Flying Horse, a drunk staggered out and started chasing it, but after a minute or so he collapsed on the ground breathing heavily. "Bugger it!" he gasped. "You can keep your bloody ice-creams."

"Whisky on the rocks, bartender, please," says the man. As he gulps it down in one go, he takes a picture from his back pocket.

"Another whisky, please," and again he gulps it down, looking at the picture from his back pocket. For the next two hours he does the same thing, time and time again. By the end of the night he turns to stagger out when the bartender taps him on the shoulder.

"Sorry, mate, but I have to ask. You've ordered whiskies all night and each time you've drunk one, you've looked at that picture. Can I ask why?"

"Shure," slurred the man. "It's a picture of my wife. When I think she's looking good, it's time for me to go home."

IN THE BUFF

How can you tell a short-sighted man in a nudist colony?
It isn't hard.

Who's the most popular man in a nudist colony?
The one who can carry two teas and a couple of doughnuts all at the same time.

A family went on holiday to the coast and wandered accidentally on to a nudist beach. The little boy ran off to play, but returned a few minutes later saying, "Mummy, Mummy, I've just seen some women with boobs much, much bigger than yours."
Mummy replied, "Son, the bigger they are, the more stupid the women."
The little boy went off again but soon came running back.
"Mummy, Mummy, I've just seen some men with much bigger willies than Daddy's."
As before, Mummy replied, "The bigger they are, the more stupid the men."

Five minutes later, and the little boy came back
very excited.
"Mummy, Mummy, I've just seen Daddy talking to the
most stupid lady I've ever seen, and as he was talking
to her, he started to get more and more stupid as well."

*A married couple decided to join a
nudist colony and, after their initial
embarrassment, they settled down
quite happily.*
*At dinner that night, the woman said to
her husband, "I'm glad we chose to do
this. It feels right, it gives me a nice
warm feeling."*
*"I'm not surprised," he replied. "You've
got your tits in the soup."*

Did you hear about the dwarf who was expelled from
the nudist colony?
He was always poking his nose into other
people's business.

WILD AT HEART

Johnson, the intrepid explorer, is making his way through the jungle, when suddenly a party of natives appears in front of him. "Hold it right there, white man!" snaps the leader. "What are you taking from the jungle?"

They search Johnson's baggage, and soon discover a large supply of walnuts.

They march him into their village, strip him naked, and tie him to a stake in the middle of the village square.

"This will teach you to steal from the jungle," says the chief, and he begins to stuff the walnuts up Johnson's a**e, saying, "This will teach you to steal our property."

On hearing this, Johnson breaks out in fits of laughter.

"How can you laugh?" demands the chief. "There must be 30lbs of walnuts here, and they're all going up your a**e. Is that funny?"

"Oh, it's not that," says Johnson, "it's just that I can't stand my boss."

"So why is that funny?" demands the chief.

"Well," says Johnson, "he's two days behind me on the trail – with a consignment of pineapples."

A man and his wife went on safari and, having lost the rest of the sightseeing party, they found themselves alone in the jungle.
Suddenly the wife screamed as they were confronted by a huge gorilla. The gorilla grabbed her by the a**e and began tearing her clothes off.
"Help, Fred, help me, what shall I do?" she yelled.
"Tell him you've got a headache and you're too tired," her husband replied.

'Not the most adventurous of hunters, was he?'

A man goes hunting with his two dogs and a monkey and his fellow hunters ask him what the monkey is for. He replies, "When the dogs have cornered the animal up a tree, the monkey goes in and shoots it at close range."
Later in the day, the dogs bark and a gun is handed to the monkey. He shins up the tree only to return a few seconds later.
He jumps to the ground and immediately shoots the dog dead.
"Christ!" exclaims one of the hunters. "Why did he do that?"
The man replied, "If there's one thing he can't stand, it's liars."

A young couple went on a safari to Africa, accompanied by the woman's mother. On the second day, they got separated from their party and found themselves in a remote part of the jungle. Suddenly, a lion jumped out of the undergrowth and stood growling ferociously in front of the mother-in-law.

"Quick, George!" screamed his wife,
"do something!"
"Not bloody likely," he replied, "that lion
got himself into this mess, he can get
himself out of it!"

Two athletes are on a safari holiday in deepest, darkest
Africa when they get separated from the rest of the
party. All of a sudden they look up to find themselves
face to face with a very angry lion. The first athlete
immediately bends down to put his running shoes on.
"What the hell are you doing?" screams the second,
"you'll never outrun him!"
"I know," says the first, "but I can outrun you."

How do you know when you've passed
a rhinoceros?
You can't close the toilet lid.

Two men on safari were cooling down by dangling their
feet in the river. Suddenly, one of them screams.

"Aaarghh, a crocodile has just bitten off my foot!"
"Which one?"
"I don't bloody know, when you've seen one, you've
seen them all."

*An elephant and a monkey were strolling
through the jungle when suddenly the
elephant fell down a large hole.
Quickly the monkey ran for help and
flagged down a Rolls-Royce on a nearby
road. Hearing of his friend's plight, the
passengers hurried to the hole, dropped
a rope down and pulled the
elephant out.
Some months later, the monkey fell
down a steep hole, but was rescued
quite easily when the elephant dropped
his donger down for the monkey to
climb up.
So it just goes to show that you don't
need a Rolls-Royce if you've got a
big d*ck.*

On safari in darkest Africa, a bishop got separated from his party and came face to face with a huge lion. Knowing his gun was empty the man got down on his knees to say a last prayer, but was amazed to find the lion praying as well.

"Praise the Lord! A Christian lion!" exclaimed the bishop joyously.

"Quiet!" roared the lion, "I'm saying grace."

'Isn't that the breed whose parents are fiercely protective?'

HOLIDAY TIME

Two young men go on holiday together to Spain and spend all day on the beach and go clubbing at night. By the time they leave the beach each day Bob has usually made a date with one of the many pretty girls round about, but Des never has any luck.

"What am I going to do? Why can't I score?" he asks Bob. His mate looks at him and says, "Tomorrow, when you come to the beach, stick an orange down your swimming trunks."

The following day, Bob is late joining Des and it's not until lunchtime that they meet up.

"Hi, Des, how's it going?"

"Still not pulled anyone," he replies dejectedly.

Bob takes another good look at him and whispers, "Next time, Des, put the orange down the **front** of your trunks."

When in Madrid, a man is recommended to go to a special local restaurant that serves the testicles of the slain bull from the local bull fight.

When he gets there, he sees written up outside the restaurant, "After the killing in the ring, the testicles are on your plate within 30 minutes."

Sitting at table, the man orders the hot testicles, but on their arrival, he is slightly disgruntled. The meal looks like two pickled walnuts covered with tomato sauce.

"This is very disappointing," he says to the waiter. "I've seen bulls' knackers and usually they're huge. What's wrong with these?"

The waiter smiles and says, "Ah yes, sir, but sometimes the bull wins."

A retired couple went away on a weekend break and couldn't find anywhere to stay. As a goodwill gesture, the manager of a four-star hotel offered to let them stay in the bridal suite.

"What the heck do we want that for? I'm 75 years old."

"Excuse me, sir, I've allowed people to stay in the snooker room before without expecting them to play snooker all night."

*"I've just had the most fabulous holiday in St Tropez," said the office girl to her friends. "I met this dishy masseur."
"You mean monsieur, don't you?" said Doreen. "A masseur is someone who gets you to strip and rubs you all over . . . "
"So this dishy masseur . . . "*

A couple staying overnight at a country hotel were unable to get to sleep because of the loud noise coming from downstairs. Eventually, the man could stand it no longer and rang down to reception.
"What the hell's going on? The noise is deafening."
"My apologies, sir, they're holding the Policeman's Ball."
"Well for f*ck's sake, tell them to let go of it!"

*A man stops overnight at a hotel and rings down to reception asking for one of their local girls.
"How disgusting," says the owner's wife.*

*"Go and tell him we don't allow that
sort of thing here."*
*But the hotel owner thought she was
making a lot of fuss about nothing.*
*"OK – I'll go and tell him," she said
and off she stormed upstairs.*
*Half an hour passed and the man
appeared downstairs and spoke to
the owner.*
*"The girls round here are a bit feisty
aren't they? The one you sent me was a
real tough one, but I got her in
the end."*

A woman from the city stops overnight at a B&B in the
heart of the country. The toilet is at the bottom of the
garden. After using it she comes back in and complains
to the owner.
"There's no lock on that toilet."
"No need," he says. "Who'd want to steal a pail
of sh*t?"

A couple and their son set up camp and the boy wandered off to play. A few minutes later he returned carrying the top half of a bikini in his hand. "Now, son," said the dad thoughtfully, "just show me exactly where you found this."

Two teachers are returning home from a two-day course when their car breaks down and they are forced to spend the night at a hotel.

Unfortunately, all the single rooms are taken so they have to share a double.

The woman gets ready for bed, changing in the bathroom, then the man does the same. Later, as they are both lying there, the woman realizes she's got the hots for her colleague, but is too shy to do anything about it. Instead, she makes idle conversation.

"Listen, Derek, it sounds as if we have a dripping tap."

Derek turns to her and replies, "I have an idea, Doreen. How about just for tonight we pretend we're man and wife?"

"Oh, yes," she says excitedly, "I'd love to."

"Good," he says, "go and turn that tap off, will you?"

Flying for the first time, an old man was having trouble with his ears, so the stewardess brought him some chewing gum. As he was leaving, he turned to her and said, "Thanks for the chewing gum, but how do I get it out of my ears?"

'They are lovely, Martha . . .
Martha? . . . '

A tourist staggers out of the bar after ten pints of beer and strays on to the nudist beach where he is confronted by a naked woman. He stands and stares at her for a few moments, until she looks up and sees him.

"What do you want?" she demands angrily.

"My wife's got an outfit just like yours," says the drunk.

A wealthy man was travelling through Egypt by camel, but had been having a lot of trouble finding a top-class animal to suit his needs.

Eventually, he was advised to visit the best camel breeder in the district, Ali Bari, who would have what he wanted.

"Good day, Ali Bari," he said. "The next stage of my trip is going to last four weeks so I need an animal that won't let me down under any circumstances. I don't care how much I pay."

"Very well," replied the dealer, and he took him to see a magnificent camel in his courtyard.

"This camel will get you there quite safely.

Just remember to give him plenty of water
before setting out."
So the wealthy man followed instructions
and then travelled into the desert. But alas,
after two weeks the camel dropped
down dead.
Fortunately, the man was rescued and was
able to finish his journey.
It wasn't until a year later that the man
found himself back in the town where he had
bought the camel. He accosted the dealer,
saying, "How dare you sell me such a poor
animal! It only lasted two weeks before
dropping dead. You swindled me."
The dealer protested, "Did you give it plenty
of water?"
"Of course I did."
"And did you give him the two-brick
treatment?"
"The two-brick treatment? What's that?"
Ali Bari replied, "When you think he's just
about to stop drinking, you bang his balls
between two bricks and he sucks in enough
water to last another two weeks."

A minicab driver had an attractive fare in the back when suddenly the engine failed. He got out and lifted the bonnet to see what was wrong. The attractive girl got out too and came over to see what he was doing.

"Do you want a screwdriver?" she asked.

"In a moment, Miss. I'll just finish up here first."

President Bush and a monkey get sent up to space to look for life on another planet. They eventually land many light years away in an unfamiliar world and each of them has an envelope with a set of instructions. The monkey opens his envelope, and inside is a thick sheaf of papers, which give him detailed instructions to study the terrain, take readings of the air pressure, rocks and minerals and finally, make contact with any alien inhabitants. George 'Dubya' opens his envelope and finds a scrap of paper which just says, "Feed the monkey, George."

There's been a severe shortage of food in the jungle, so when a missionary appears, two cannibals start to fight over who will take the prize. Eventually, too weak to argue, they decide to share him – one starting at the top, the other at his feet, until they meet up in the middle. After eating for some minutes, one cannibal turns to the other and says, "How's it going?"
"Fantastic!" replies the other. "I'm having a ball."
"Oh, no!" exclaims the first, "slow down, you're eating too fast!"

'Why can't you just go for a swim like everybody else?'

RETAIL THERAPY

The man knocked on his manager's door.
"Excuse me, sir, may I have tomorrow off? The wife
wants to go shopping."
"Certainly not," replied the manager.
"Oh, thank you, sir, you've saved my life!"

*A bloke goes into a baker's and asks
for three pork pies. The assistant picks
the pies up with a pair of tongs and
puts them in a paper bag. The man then
asks for three strawberry tarts and the
assistant picks up another pair of tongs
and puts three tarts into a bag.
"I must compliment you on such
impressive hygienic standards," says
the man.
"Thank you," said the assistant. "We're
very careful not to touch any of
the food."
Just as the man is leaving the shop, he*

notices a piece of string hanging from the assistant's trousers.
"Excuse me, what is that piece of string?" he asked.
"That's used when I go to the toilet. So that I don't touch my penis, I pull it out with the string," said the assistant.
"But how do you put it back?"
"Oh, I use one of these pairs of tongs."

There was only one supermarket basket left at the door of the shop as a woman and a man approached from separate directions.

"Excuse me," said the woman, "do you want that basket?"

"No, thanks," he replied, "I'm only after one thing."

"Typical male," she said to herself as he walked away.

Coming home from work, a man passed a sex shop and on impulse went in and bought a blow-up doll. He couldn't wait to get home to try it out, but when he pumped her up, she just went flat again. The next day the man went back to the sex shop and demanded to see the manager.

"So what exactly was wrong with the doll?" he asked.

"I'll tell you what," he replied angrily. "As soon as I'd blown her up, she went down on me."

"Bloody hell," exclaimed the manager. "If I'd known that, I'd have charged you twice as much!"

A man goes to the most exclusive shop in Mayfair to buy his wife some exquisite lingerie for their wedding anniversary.

The sales assistant shows him some outfits around £100, but he shakes his head, saying, "No, it's got to be more sheer than that."

She then shows him an outfit at £150, but he insists on having something even more sheer. So eventually she brings out some lingerie at £400, extra extra sheer.

He takes the lingerie home and asks his wife to go and put it on so that he can see what it looks like. The wife, however, decides to play a trick on him. She is convinced it is so sheer that he won't be able to tell whether she is wearing it or not. She decides to take it back to the shop and pocket the refund.

So she appears before him with nothing on.

"Well, what do you think?" she says.

"Crikey!" he replies. "You'd think at that price they'd iron out the creases first."

A Scotsman, a bit the worse for wear, staggered into an off-licence for some more booze. There were two men in front of him. The first had a huge beard and a big cigar. He ordered hundreds

of pounds worth of spirits and told the shop assistant to put it on the F11 convention bill. After he had gone the second man, also sporting a large cigar and a slightly smaller beard, ordered £200 of sherry and port, and asked for it also to be put on the F11 convention account.

So the Scotsman thought he'd try and get away with the same thing.

"Two crates of whisky, please, and put it on the F11 convention account, my good man," he said, trying to sound very upright and sober. The shop assistant replied, "I'm sorry, sir, I can't do that, you don't have a large beard and a cigar."

For a moment the Scotsman looked defeated, but then a smile lit up his face as he lifted his kilt and replied, "Ah, yes, but I'm working undercover."